머리말

1990년대 이후부터 우리나라 영어 교육에서 청취력에 관한 관심이 학교의 현장 교육, 교재 개발 및 평가 반영 등의 분야에서 높게 나타나고 있음에도 불구하고 청취에 관련된 기본 지침서나 교재 등이 부족했던 것이 현실이다. 더욱이 TOEFL과 관련된 초·중급 수준 교재의 빈약함에 대한 학습자들의 고충을 덜어보려는 노력으로 LinguaForum Research Center에서는 초·중급용 청취 교재를 개발하게 되었다.

청취는 짧은 시간 내에 일정한 실력을 쌓기가 쉽지 않은 일이긴 하지만, 훌륭한 방법론을 제시한 좋은 교재로 학습해 나간다면 못할 일도 아니다. 청취는 영어의 다른 분야와 마찬가지로 매일 학습하는 것이 필요하며, 가능하다면 청취에 항상 개방된 자세와 환경의 유지가 무엇보다도 필요하다.

이번에 새로운 디자인과 구성으로 개정한 링구아포럼 iBT e TOEFL Listening은 초급 수준에 최적화된 교재로서 TOEFL 청취 전반을 학습할 수 있도록 구성하였다. 특히 iBT TOEFL 문제 유형의 개념 정리부터 실전용 Test에 이르기까지 흐름을 알기 쉽게 정리해 놓았다.

아무쪼록 링구아포럼에서 만든 본 교재가 학습자들의 기본적인 영어 이해 능력과 의사소통 능력 신장에 도움을 주고 독자들이 소기의 목적을 이룰 수 있다면, 더할 나위 없는 보람으로 여기며 보다 나은 책을 만들어 내는데 정진 할 것을 약속한다.

LinguaForum Research Center
청취 연구팀

각 장의 구성

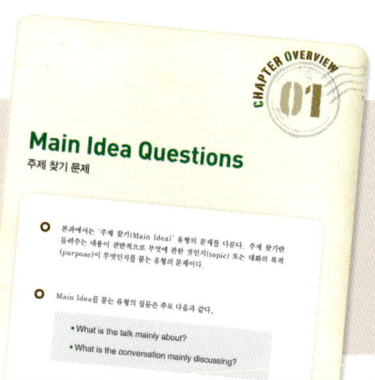

Overview

*i*BT TOEFL의 각 문제 유형에 대한 중요 사항을 설명하며 문제 풀이에 필요한 정보를 제공한다.

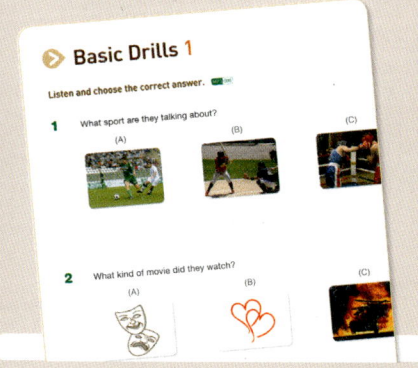

Basic Drills

본격적인 청취 연습에 앞서 각 장에서 소개한 문제 유형에 대한 기본 개념을 연습한다. 사진이나 그림 등과 함께 짧은 글을 통해 연습해 볼 수 있다.

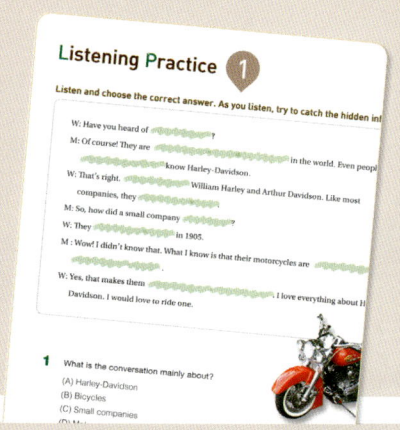

Listening Practice

다양한 내용의 청취 지문을 통해 본격적으로 청취 연습을 해본다.
① 중요 정보가 가려진 지문을 보면서 듣고 푸는 문제, ② 지문을 모두 듣고 푸는 문제 유형으로 연습되어진다.

LinguaForum

기획	링구아포럼 기획편집팀			
지은이	링구아포럼 리서치센터 연구팀			
디자인	링구아포럼 디자인팀			
편집인	최인호			
발행인	이길호			
발행처	링구아포럼			
교재문의	02) 3480-6613	대표전화 02) 590-6900		
등록번호	제2000-000335호	등록일자 2000. 5. 17	ISBN 978-89-5563-616-1 (14740)	가격 17,000원

Copyright ⓒ 2010-2011 by LinguaForum

No unauthorized photocopying.
All rights reserved. No part of this book may be reproduced or transmitted in any form or by any means, electronic or mechanical, including photocopying, recording, or any other information storage and retrieval system without the written permission of the publisher.
이 책은 링구아포럼이 독창적으로 개발하였습니다. 이 책의 내용, 사진 등 일부 혹은 전체 내용을 어떠한 방법으로도 무단 복사, 복제, 전재하는 것은 저작권법에 의해 금지되어 있습니다.

Printed in the Republic of Korea

R/N(CReTFLneG): 09071030KB / 10221030KB / 01141130KB / 10051130KB

*i*BT Practice

실제 토플 시험과 같은 구성의 문제를 풀어 보면서 실력을 점검하고 실전에 대비한다. 단, Organization-Rhetorical Connection 유형과 Content-Linking 유형은 추론 (Inference) 문제 유형으로 e TOEFL Listening에서는 다루지 않고 다음 단계인 b TOEFL Listening에서 다루게 된다.

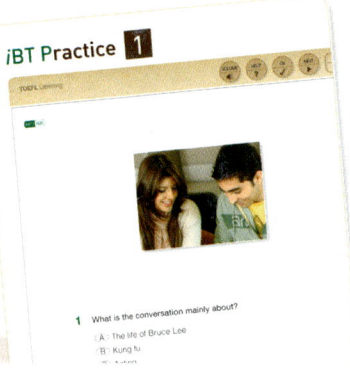

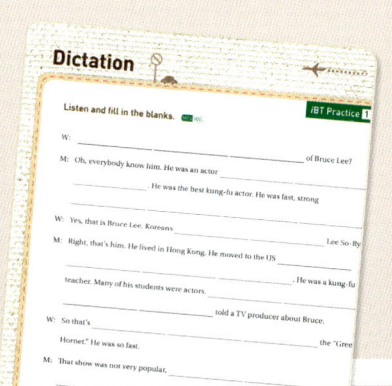

Dictation

받아쓰기는 청취력 향상을 위한 필수적인 연습 방법이다. *i*BT Practice 에서 나온 지문을 다시 한번 듣고 받아 쓰는 연습을 통해 들리지 않고 이해되지 않았던 부분이 어디인지를 확인해본다.

Word Review

청취 능력뿐만 아니라 언어 능력 향상을 좌우하는 중요 요소 중의 하나인 어휘와 주요 표현을 정리한다. 각 장에서 사용되었던 중요 어휘와 표현을 문제를 통해 다시 한번 복습한다.

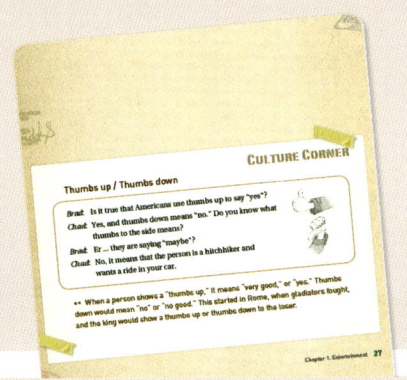

Culture Corner

영어가 갖는 독특한 표현들이나 미국의 문화, 풍속 등에 대한 설명과 상황별 대화를 익히고 실생활에서 활용해 본다.

Contents

Chapter 1
Topic **Entertainment** — 8
Question Type **Main Idea**

Overview — 10
Basic Drills — 12
Listening Practice — 14
iBT Practice — 18
Dictation — 22
Word Review — 26

Chapter 2
Topic **Jobs** — 28
Question Type **Supporting Detail**

Overview — 30
Basic Drills — 32
Listening Practice — 34
iBT Practice — 38
Dictation — 42
Word Review — 46

Chapter 3
Topic **Do's & Don'ts** — 48
Question Type **Organization**

Overview — 50
Basic Drills — 52
Listening Practice — 54
iBT Practice — 58
Dictation — 62
Word Review — 66

Chapter **4**	Topic **Technology**	68
	Question Type **Content-Identifying Relationship**	

Overview 70
Basic Drills 72
Listening Practice 74
*i*BT Practice 78
Dictation 82
Word Review 86

Chapter **5**	Topic **History**	88
	Question Type **Stance / Attitude**	

Overview 90
Basic Drills 92
Listening Practice 94
*i*BT Practice 98
Dictation 102
Word Review 106

Chapter **6**	Topic **Biography**	108
	Question Type **Function-Purpose**	

Overview 110
Basic Drills 112
Listening Practice 114
*i*BT Practice 118
Dictation 122
Word Review 126

Mini Test 1-3   128
Scripts & Answer Key

Chapter 1
Entertainment

Linguaforum e-Listening

Chapter 1

Topic:
Entertainment

Question Type:

Main Idea Questions
주제 찾기 문제
글의 전반적인 내용을 파악하는 문제

Main Idea Questions
주제 찾기 문제

○ 본과에서는 '주제 찾기(Main Idea)' 유형의 문제를 다룬다. 주제 찾기란 들려주는 내용이 전반적으로 무엇에 관한 것인지(topic) 또는 대화의 목적(purpose)이 무엇인지를 묻는 유형의 문제이다.

○ Main Idea를 묻는 유형의 질문은 주로 다음과 같다.

- What is the talk mainly about?
- What is the conversation mainly discussing?

Sample Question

TOEFL Listening

What is the talk mainly about?

- Ⓐ Reasons to go to a concert
- Ⓑ Bad points of concerts
- Ⓒ Bringing flowers and posters to concerts
- Ⓓ Singers in concerts

Script & 해석

Many teenagers like to go to music concerts. Concerts allow fans to meet their favorite stars. Fans bring many things to a concert. They bring lights, balloons, flowers and posters. The fans want to show their support. They also want to give the flowers to the singer or group. Concerts are good for releasing stress. People can scream and jump around in concerts. Screaming and having fun in concerts lower stress. Singers also like to perform. They are very happy when many people come to see them.

많은 십대청소년들은 음악 콘서트에 가는 것을 좋아한다. 콘서트에서 팬들은 그들이 좋아하는 스타들을 만날 수 있다. 팬들은 콘서트에 많은 것들을 가지고 온다. 그들은 조명, 풍선, 꽃, 포스터 등을 가지고 온다. 팬들은 그들이 격려하는걸 보여주고 싶어한다. 그들은 또한 가수나 그룹에게 꽃을 주고 싶어한다. 콘서트는 스트레스를 풀기에 좋다. 콘서트 중에 사람들은 소리지르고 뛰어다닐 수 있다. 콘서트 중에 소리를 지르며 즐기는 동안 스트레스가 줄어든다. 가수들 역시 공연을 하고 싶어한다. 많은 팬들이 그들을 보러 올 때 행복해 한다.

Basic Drills 1

Listen and choose the correct answer. MP3 3-5

1 What sport are they talking about?

(A) 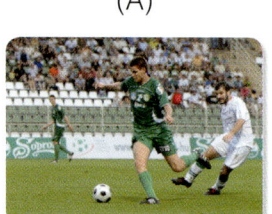 (B)  (C)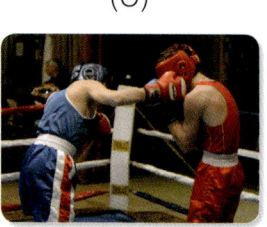

2 What kind of movie did they watch?

(A)  (B)  (C)

3 What are they talking about?

(A)  (B)  (C)

Basic Drills 2

Listen and choose the correct answer. MP3 6-8

1

What is the talk about?

(A) Uses of the internet
(B) Playing games

2

What is the talk about?

(A) Fun sports
(B) Inline Skating safety

3

What is the conversation about?

(A) Television
(B) *Titanic*

Listening Practice 1

Listen and choose the correct answer. As you listen, try to catch the hidden information.

Many people ~~~~~ on television and ~~~~~ are getting more popular every day. However, ~~~~~.

There are ~~~~~. The most common are called ~~~~~. They only talk ~~~~~.

Comedians have to ~~~~~ and write new jokes. They ~~~~~ and make sure that ~~~~~ to a broad audience. If they are not ~~~~~ them. This is a comedian's ~~~~~.

The next time we see comedians, remember that ~~~~~. Let's laugh a little louder for them.

1 What is the talk about?

(A) Funny comedians
(B) Sad comedians
(C) Easy life of comedians
(D) Hard life of comedians

2 According to the passage, what do comedians study?

(A) They study about other comedians.
(B) They study about nightmares.
(C) They study about comic books.
(D) They study about television.

Listening Practice 2

Listen and choose the correct answer. As you listen, try to catch the hidden information.

W: Look at ＿＿＿＿＿. They are going to fall!

M: Calm down. It's all ＿＿＿.

W: Are you sure? They look like ＿＿＿. They have ＿＿＿, and it looks like ＿＿＿.

M: I'm sure they have ＿＿＿. The bucket is ＿＿＿. I am sure it is ＿＿＿ like that.

W: But it looks ＿＿. The clowns look like they are ＿＿＿. I don't want to ＿＿.

M: So you still think ＿＿? I guess the clowns have ＿＿＿.

1 What is the conversation mainly about?

(A) The audience at the show
(B) The clowns in the show
(C) A bucket of water
(D) Dangerous clowns

2 What are the clowns riding?

(A) A motorcycle
(B) A car
(C) A bicycle
(D) A train

Listening Practice 3

Listen and choose the correct answer.

MP3 11

memo

1 What is the talk mainly about?

(A) New rides
(B) Slow rides
(C) Fastest ride
(D) Long rides

2 Where can we enjoy the rides?

(A) In the museum
(B) In the street
(C) On the ground
(D) In amusement parks

Listening Practice 4

Listen and choose the correct answer.

memo

1 What is the talk mainly about?

(A) Mickey Mouse
(B) Fun in Disneyland
(C) Los Angeles
(D) Light show

2 What can we enjoy at night in Disneyland?

(A) Meeting Donald Duck
(B) Getting on fun rides
(C) Taking pictures
(D) Watching the light parade

iBT Practice 1

TOEFL Listening

1 What is the conversation mainly about?

- Ⓐ The life of Bruce Lee
- Ⓑ Kung fu
- Ⓒ Acting
- Ⓓ Green Hornet

2 Who was Bruce Lee?

- Ⓐ A TV producer
- Ⓑ A student
- Ⓒ An actor
- Ⓓ A Korean

3 What is the conversation mainly about?

  Ⓐ Seoul Land
  Ⓑ A zoo
  Ⓒ Animals
  Ⓓ Flowers

4 Which restaurant does the woman introduce?

  Ⓐ A Chinese restaurant
  Ⓑ A hamburger shop
  Ⓒ A salad bar
  Ⓓ A Korean restaurant

iBT Practice 2

1 What is the talk mainly about?

- Ⓐ Pop music
- Ⓑ Latin music
- Ⓒ Drama
- Ⓓ Rap

2 What are rappers sometimes called?

- Ⓐ Dancers
- Ⓑ Poets
- Ⓒ Pop stars
- Ⓓ Boy bands

3 What is the conversation about?

    Ⓐ The jokes of the comedian
    Ⓑ Two friends
    Ⓒ An unhappy mother
    Ⓓ The girl's mother

4 According to the conversation, what do comedians do?

    Ⓐ They make fun of others.
    Ⓑ They make fun of themselves.
    Ⓒ Mothers make fun of comedians.
    Ⓓ They make people angry.

Dictation

iBT Practice 1 1-2

Listen and fill in the blanks. MP3 13

W: _____ _____ _____ of Bruce Lee?

M: Oh, everybody knows him. He was an actor _____ _____ _____. He was the best kung-fu actor. He was fast, strong _____ _____ _____ _____.

W: Yes, that is Bruce Lee. Koreans _____ _____ Lee So-Ryong.

M: Right, that's him. He lived in Hong Kong. He moved to the US _____ _____ _____ _____. He was a kung-fu teacher. Many of his students were actors. _____ _____ _____ _____ told a TV producer about Bruce.

W: So that's _____ _____ _____ the "Green Hornet." He was so fast.

M: That show was not very popular, _____ _____ _____ _____ Bruce very famous. Later, he went to Hong Kong, but he only made a few movies. He died _____ _____ _____.

iBT Practice 1 3-4

Listen and fill in the blanks. MP3 14

M: We are going to Seoul Land _____ _____. We will bring our dog, Mimi, too. _____ _____ _____ _____ told me that there are many kinds of flowers.

W: Yes, the park is covered with flowers _____ _____. If you go there, visit the zoo _____ _____.

M: _____ _____ _____ _____ are in the zoo?

W: Tigers, lions, elephants, bears ... but don't worry. They are _____ _____ _____.

M: What about birds? I love birds.

W: Sure, you can also see _____ _____ _____.

M: Great! Do you know any nice restaurants in Seoul Land?

W: Yes, there is a delicious Korean restaurant _____ _____ _____. They serve rice and vegetables _____ _____ _____. Their meat and fish dishes are good too. _____ _____ you go there.

iBT Practice 2 1-2

Listen and fill in the blanks. MP3 15

Rap was _____ _____ _____ new music in the 1990s. Black music has always been important _____ _____ _____ of pop music. Rap is different _____ _____ _____. It is because rap singers talk _____ _____ _____ _____. They speak their words fast over music. Their words are _____ _____. They always rhyme with the next line. This is why rap singers _____ _____ _____ poets.

Musicians take sounds from different records _____ _____ _____ for their lyrics. Rap was the music _____ _____ _____ _____. The words were about hard life in the city. Rap changed pop music _____ _____ _____.

iBT Practice 2 3-4

Listen and fill in the blanks. MP3 16

W: Can you believe that guy? He wasn't funny _____ _____.

M: Really? I _____ _____ laughing! His jokes were very funny.

W: I don't think it's funny. He _____ _____ _____ about his own mother _____ _____.

M: That's what stand-up comedians do. They _____ _____ _____ _____ and copy other people.

W: Well, _____ _____ _____ about your own mother is bad. Telling other people about it is worse.

M: Don't be _____ _____. Everybody knows it was _____ _____ _____. I'm sure his mother understands.

W: I know, but my mom wouldn't be happy _____ _____ _____ _____.

M: That is because you are not a comedian. If you were a comedian, I am sure your mom _____ _____, too.

Match the words from the box with the definitions.

| release | perform | empty | scream |
| ride | decorate | cage | poet |

1 _____ with no people or things inside

2 _____ to cry loudly because you are hurt, frightened, or excited

3 _____ to make something look more attractive by putting things on it

4 _____ a box of wire or metal bars for keeping birds or animals in

5 _____ a machine at an amusement park that people ride in for fun

6 _____ to do something in front of an audience in order to entertain them

7 _____ to allow to leave; to get rid of a negative feeling

8 _____ someone who writes poems

Choose the best phrase to fit in each one of the blanks.

| calm down | make sure | shook hands | made fun of |

9 To _____ we arrived on time, we left home early.

10 When he first moved to the US, some people _____ his accent.

11 After hearing bad news, she had to _____ and think carefully.

12 The two businessmen _____ to show they had a deal.

Culture Corner

Thumbs up / Thumbs down

Brad: Is it true that Americans use thumbs up to say "yes"?

Chad: Yes, and thumbs down means "no." Do you know what thumbs to the side means?

Brad: Er ... they are saying "maybe"?

Chad: No, it means that the person is a hitchhiker and wants a ride in your car.

•• When a person shows a "thumbs up," it means "very good," or "yes." Thumbs down would mean "no" or "no good." This started in Rome, when gladiators fought, and the king would show a thumbs up or thumbs down to the loser.

Chapter 1. Entertainment

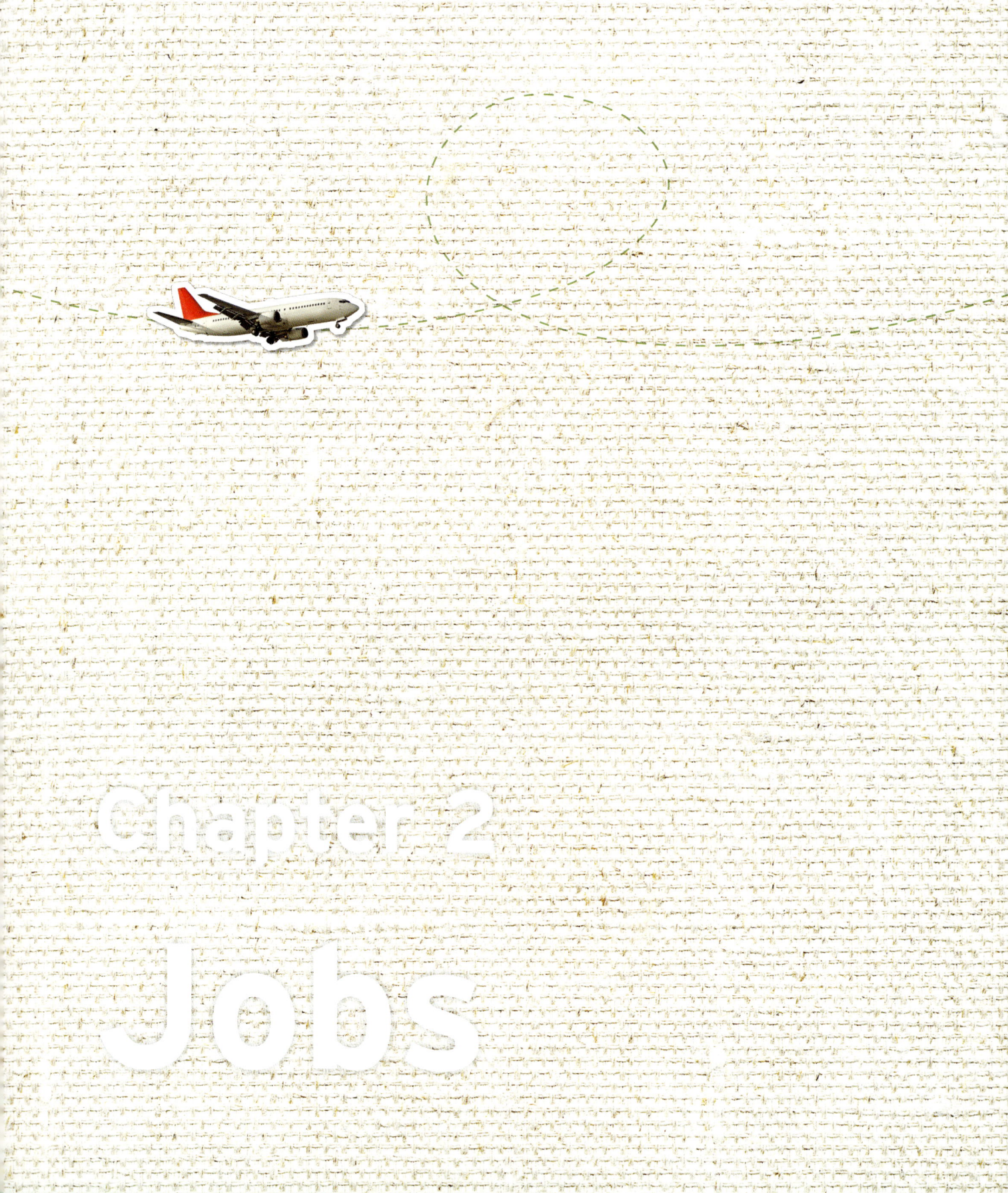

Chapter 2
Jobs

Chapter 2

Topic:

Jobs

Question Type:

Supporting Detail Questions

세부 사항 문제

글의 중요 세부 사항을 파악하는 문제

Supporting Detail Questions
세부 사항 문제

○ 본과에서는 '세부 사항(Supporting Detail)' 찾기 유형의 문제를 다룬다. 세부사항 찾기란 들려주는 대화나 글의 내용 중에서 언급된 중요 세부 사항(important detail)에 대해 묻는 형태의 문제이다.
  • 한 개 이상의 답을 요구하는 유형의 문제도 있다.

○ Supporting Detail을 묻는 유형의 질문은 주로 다음과 같다.

> • According to the teacher, what do nurses do?
>
> • According to the conversation, what is true about firefighters?

Sample Question

According to the speaker, what must singers do?

Ⓐ Singers must have a lot of rest.
Ⓑ Singers must know how to dance.
Ⓒ Singers must practice meeting fans.
Ⓓ Singers must sing with fans.

Script & 해석

It is not easy to be a singer. Singers work very hard. Singers must sing in concerts and television shows and meet fans. They travel to many places for concerts. Some singers even travel to another country. They have very little time to rest. Singers must also know how to dance. They must practice for many hours though they are tired. This is because people think it is boring to see singers stand and sing, so stars must dance on stage.

가수가 되는 것은 쉬운 일이 아니다. 가수들은 아주 힘들게 일한다. 가수들은 콘서트, 텔레비전 쇼 프로에서 노래를 해야 하고 팬들도 만나야 한다. 그들은 공연을 하기 위해 여러 곳으로 여행을 다닌다. 어떤 가수들은 심지어 다른 나라로 공연하러 가기도 한다. 그들은 쉴 시간이 거의 없다. 가수들은 춤도 출 줄 알아야 한다. 피곤하더라도 몇 시간 동안 연습을 해야 한다. 사람들은 가수가 서서 노래하는 것이 지루하다고 생각하기 때문에 스타들은 무대 위에서 춤을 춰야만 한다.

Basic Drills 1

Listen and choose the correct answer. MP3 18-20

1 When is she going to start her job?

(A)  (B)  (C)

2 What fruit did the man move?

(A)  (B)  (C)

3 What does Sally travel with?

(A) 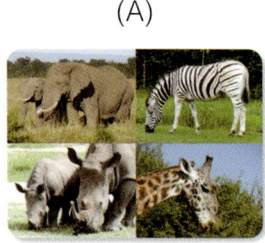 (B)  (C)

Basic Drills 2

Listen and choose the correct answer. MP3 21-23

1

What can we do at home to get money?

(A) Cut the grass
(B) Sleep

2

Which kind of job is quiet and safe?

(A) Outdoor jobs
(B) Jobs in the office

3

Why do dancers need a lot of energy?

(A) Dancers need a lot of practice.
(B) Dancers perform in private.

Listening Practice 1

Listen and choose the correct answer. As you listen, try to catch the hidden information.

W: Have you heard of ~~~~~~~~?

M: Of course! They are ~~~~~~~~~~~~~~~~~~~~ in the world. Even people ~~~~~~~~~~~~~~~~~~~~ know Harley-Davidson.

W: That's right. ~~~~~~~~~ William Harley and Arthur Davidson. Like most companies, they ~~~~~~~~~.

M: So, how did a small company ~~~~~~~~?

W: They ~~~~~~~~ in 1905.

M: Wow! I didn't know that. What I know is that their motorcycles are ~~~~~~~~~~~~~~~~~~~.

W: Yes, that makes them ~~~~~~~~~~~~~~~~. I love everything about Harley-Davidson. I would love to ride one.

1 What is the conversation mainly about?

(A) Harley-Davidson
(B) Bicycles
(C) Small companies
(D) Motorcycle races

2 What is special about the motorcycles?

(A) They won a race.
(B) They make good sounds.
(C) They started off small.
(D) They made motorcycles.

Listening Practice 2

Listen and choose the correct answer. As you listen, try to catch the hidden information.

W: Who do you think is ~~_____~~ ?

M: I say it's Evel Knievel. He was ~~_____~~ in the US.

W: Yes, I heard of him. He was that guy on the motorcycle, right? ~~_____~~ ~~_____~~ ?

M: It was probably because he ~~_____~~. He also ~~_____~~ a lot. He ~~_____~~ after he landed when ~~_____~~ of a 41-meter jump.

W: How badly did he ~~_____~~ ?

M: Well, he ~~_____~~ in his life as a stuntman.

W: Yes, I remember hearing that he once had to ~~_____~~. He still did jumps after that.

1 What is the conversation mainly about?

(A) Broken bones
(B) Stuntmen's danger
(C) Evel Knievel
(D) Motorcycles

2 What was different from Evel Knievel and other stuntmen?

(A) He rode motorcycles.
(B) He did the longest jumps.
(C) He went to a hospital.
(D) He did not jump after he got hurt.

Listening Practice 3

Listen and choose the correct answer.

memo

1 What is the talk mainly about?

(A) Popularity of sumo wrestling
(B) Size of sumo wrestlers
(C) The Grand Champion of sumo
(D) Rules of sumo wrestling

2 How often do sumo wrestlers choose a new Grand Champion?

(A) Every day
(B) Every month
(C) Every year
(D) Every two years

Listening Practice 4

Listen and choose the correct answer.

MP3 27

memo

1 What is the conversation mainly about?

(A) Tricky law
(B) Good and bad lawyers
(C) Hunting sharks
(D) Fighting by law

2 According to the conversation, what do lawyers do?

(A) Lawyers do not help poor people.
(B) Lawyers only look for money.
(C) Lawyers do not understand the law.
(D) Lawyers fight using law.

Chapter 2. Jobs 37

iBT Practice 1

TOEFL Listening

1. What is the conversation mainly about?

    Ⓐ Helping doctors
    Ⓑ Reasons to become a doctor
    Ⓒ Going to a doctor
    Ⓓ News of a patient

2. According to the conversation, when do doctors feel good about themselves? Tick in the correct box.

	Yes	No
Ⓐ Helping patients get better		
Ⓑ Getting a lot of money		
Ⓒ Telling family and friends of patients good news		
Ⓓ Being busy all the time		

3 What is the talk mainly about?

    Ⓐ Importance of nurses

    Ⓑ Doctors and nurses

    Ⓒ Doctors in a hospital

    Ⓓ Machines in the operating room

4 According to the teacher, what do nurses do?

    Ⓐ They serve food to the patient.

    Ⓑ They concentrate on the operation.

    Ⓒ They help doctors in the operating room.

    Ⓓ They do not check on the patient.

iBT Practice 2

TOEFL Listening

1 What is the teacher mainly talking about?

- Ⓐ Flying the airplanes
- Ⓑ Training and importance of pilots
- Ⓒ Listening to pilots in an emergency
- Ⓓ Computers of airplanes

2 According to the teacher, what must pilots do before each flight?

- Ⓐ Pilots must eat special food.
- Ⓑ Pilots must check the people.
- Ⓒ Pilots must train just before flying the plane.
- Ⓓ Pilots must check the inside and outside of the airplane.

3 What is the talk mainly about?

Ⓐ Selling newspapers
Ⓑ A large-sized shop
Ⓒ Working in a small shop
Ⓓ Easy work in a shop

4 According to the student, when does her aunt sell ice cream the most?

Ⓐ In the morning
Ⓑ In the afternoon
Ⓒ In the evening
Ⓓ At night

Dictation

 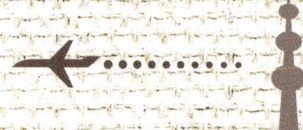

iBT Practice 1 1-2

Listen and fill in the blanks. MP3 28

W: Is it good _____ _____ _____ _____?

M: _____ _____ _____ good and bad. Being a doctor, I have many responsibilities, _____ _____ _____ _____ that I am happy to be a doctor.

M: When are you happy _____ _____ _____? Doctors seem to be busy all the time.

M: You are right. We are always busy. When people need help, they come to us. We help them _____ _____ _____. Helping people can feel good.

W: Is that all? I thought it was good _____ _____ _____.

M: I don't think so. We become doctors because we want _____ _____ _____.

W: _____ _____ makes you happy being a doctor?

M: When we tell family and friends _____ _____ _____ about a patient, it is a great feeling.

iBT Practice 1 3-4

Listen and fill in the blanks. MP3 29

There are many nurses _____ _____ _____. They seem to be everywhere. Did you know that there are nurses even in the operating room? _____ _____, doctors need very clean hands for the operation. This is why nurses _____ _____ many things.

During the operation, doctors concentrate _____ _____ _____ nurses must concentrate on the machines _____ _____ _____ about the patient. Nurses play _____ _____ _____ in the operating room.

After the operation, nurses stay _____ _____ _____. They make sure that the patient is doing OK. Nurses check on the patient often until the patient leaves the hospital. _____ _____ _____ to thank the nurses next time.

iBT Practice 2 1-2

Listen and fill in the blanks. MP3 30

Many people _____ in airplanes. But not many people know _____ _____ _____ a big plane. Pilots know _____ _____ _____ the airplane. They train very hard to become a pilot. Pilots _____ _____ for everyone in the plane.

Before each flight, pilots check the inside _____ _____ of the plane. They must make sure that there is _____ _____ with the plane.

Pilots train for many different problems. This is why everyone _____ _____ _____ in an emergency. Pilots are the most important people _____ _____ _____. They must not get sick when flying the plane, so they eat food _____ _____ _____ _____ for them.

Do you want to become a pilot _____ _____?

iBT Practice 2 3-4

Listen and fill in the blanks. MP3 31

    My aunt has a small shop _____ _____ _____ _____ _____.

She sells many things in such a small space — drinks, newspapers, food, and snacks — _____ _____! People are always buying something, so she is _____ _____.

    In the morning, a lot of people buy newspapers. Some people _____ _____ _____ their bus pass. Some people buy sandwiches _____ _____. When school _____ _____ in the afternoon, a lot of students buy ice cream and snacks. They buy food _____ _____ _____ _____ back home, or on the way to an institute. In the evening, a lot of people from the office _____ _____ _____ drinks and chewing gum.

    My aunt can only rest when she _____ _____ _____. It must be so tiring to sell things every day for so long! But my aunt says that she enjoys working _____ _____ _____.

Match the words from the box with the definitions.

| neighbor | professional | land | lawyer |
| responsibility | protect | prepare | emergency |

1. _____ to keep someone or something from being harmed or damaged

2. _____ an unexpected, serious situation that requires immediate action

3. _____ someone whose job is to provide people with legal advice and services

4. _____ someone who lives next door or nearby

5. _____ to come down to the ground after a flight or jump

6. _____ someone who has a lot of skill or training

7. _____ to make something ready for use

8. _____ a duty that you have because of your job or position

Choose the best phrase to fit in each one of the blanks.

| look for | in public | for free | on the way |

9. The letter is _____ to you and should arrive tomorrow.

10. The store gives out samples of the product _____ in order to introduce it to consumers.

11. The candidates for mayor had a debate _____, where everyone could listen.

12. To _____ names and addresses, we performed an online search.

Culture Corner

Saying "Bless you" when sneezing

Bob: Aaaah chooo!
Mr. Jones: Bless you.
Bob: Thank you. I think I really need that blessing. My cold is getting worse.

•• Long ago, people said "Bless you" to anyone that sneezed because they thought sneezing would make the soul leave the body. We know that is not true, but we still say it because it is polite.

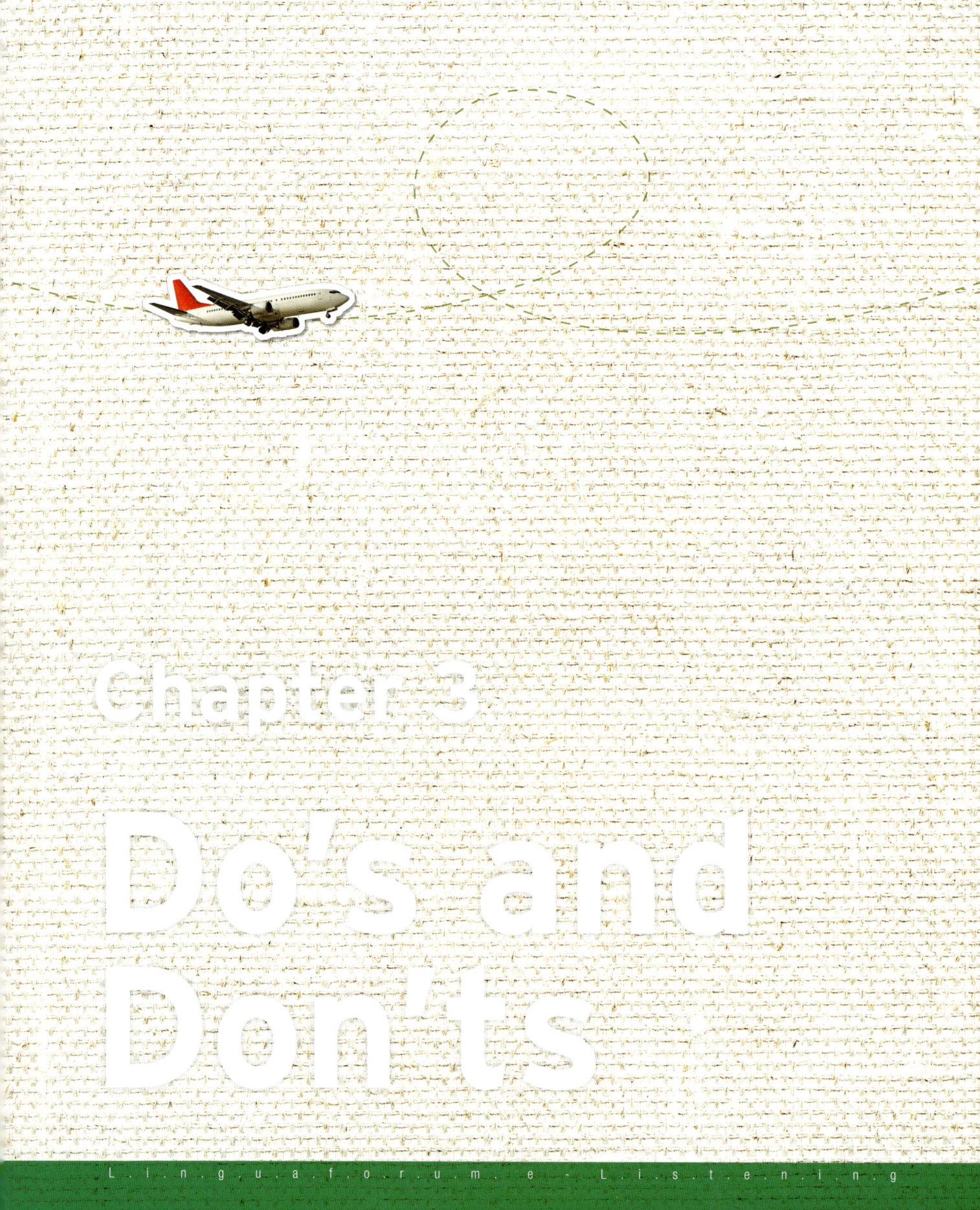

Chapter 3
Do's and Don'ts

Chapter 3

Topic:
Do's and Don'ts

Question Type:
Organization Questions
구성 인식 문제
글의 전체 구성을 파악하는 문제

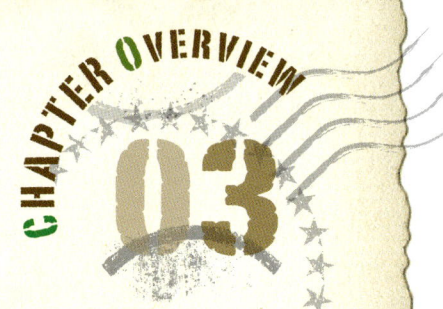

Organization Questions
구성 인식 문제

- 본과에서는 '구성(Organization) 인식' 문제를 다룬다. 구성 인식 문제란 들려 주는 글의 전체 구성(organization)을 파악하는 능력을 확인하는 유형의 문제이다. 말하는 사람은 자신의 의견이나 정보를 효과적으로 전달하기 위하여 예시(example), 사실 열거(list), 비교(comparison), 대조(contrast), 또는 시간 순서(time order) 등의 다양한 구성 방식을 활용할 수 있다는 것을 알아 두자.

- Organization과 관련된 문제를 묻는 유형의 질문은 주로 다음과 같다.

  > - How does the speaker tell us that college is important?
  > - In what order does the teacher tell us about the good points of exercising?

Sample Question

TOEFL Listening

How does the teacher speak about the rules of soccer?

Ⓐ He lists the basics of the game.
Ⓑ He compares the rules with other sports.
Ⓒ He names a few soccer teams.
Ⓓ He gives reasons why we need rules in soccer.

Script & 해석

If you want to play soccer, you must know a few easy rules. First, you cannot touch the ball with your hands. You can only use your head and your legs. Second, you have to keep the ball inside the lines. Third, you must start over after each goal. After each goal, the other team gets the ball. Finally, the game is over after ninety minutes of play. The team with the higher score is the winner.

축구를 하고 싶다면 몇 가지 간단한 규칙을 알아야 한다. 첫째, 손으로 공을 만져서는 안 된다. 오로지 머리와 다리만을 이용할 수 있다. 둘째, 공을 항상 선 안 쪽에 두어야 한다. 셋째, 득점 후에는 경기를 다시 시작해야 한다. 득점 후에는 상대편 팀이 공을 갖는다. 마지막으로, 경기는 90분 진행 후 종료된다. 점수가 높은 팀이 이기는 것이다.

▶ Basic Drills 1

Listen and choose the correct answer. MP3 33-35

1 In what order did they spend their days in camp?

(A)　　　　　　　　(B)　　　　　　　　(C)

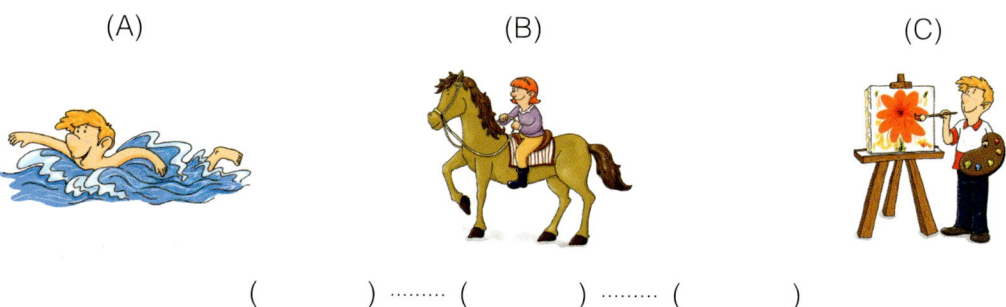

(　　) ……… (　　) ……… (　　)

2 In what order can you get your license?

(A)　　　　　　　　(B)　　　　　　　　(C)

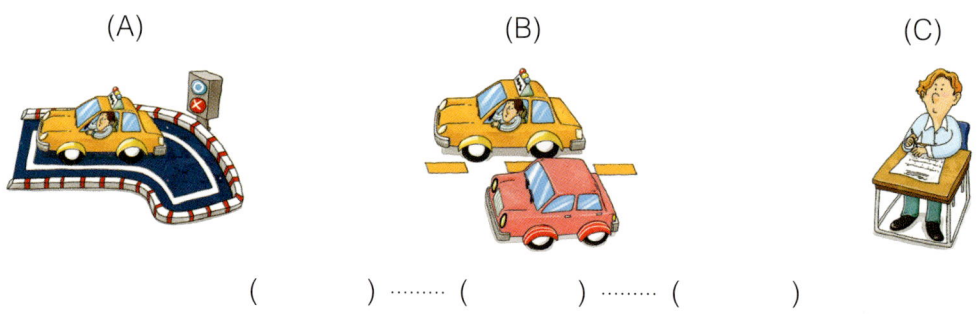

(　　) ……… (　　) ……… (　　)

3 Which fruit was NOT compared?

(A)　　　　　　　　(B)　　　　　　　　(C)

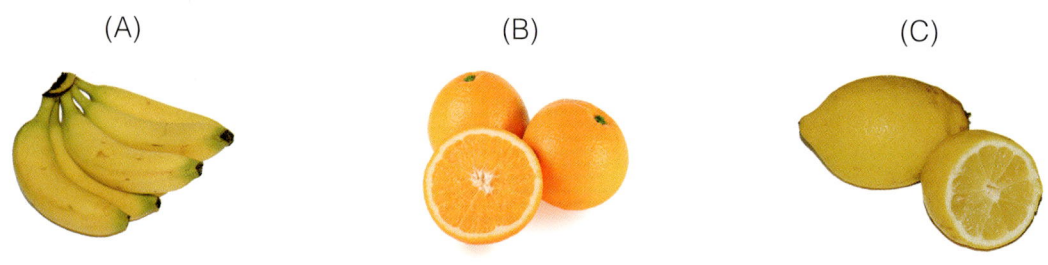

*citric acid: 신맛을 내는 산의 일종

Basic Drills 2

Listen and choose the correct answer. MP3 36-38

1

How does the speaker talk about the importance of breakfast?

(A) By time order of meals
(B) By comparing with other meals

2

How does the camp instructor tell us about camping?

(A) By giving examples
(B) By comparing camps

3

How does the speaker tell us the importance of safety on a mountain?

(A) By contrasting a good and a bad climber
(B) By giving examples of what can happen

Listening Practice 1

Listen and choose the correct answer. As you listen, try to catch the hidden information.

Many of us ~~~~~. We must also remember ~~~~~. Table manners are important in any culture, and ~~~~~.

First, when food enters our mouth, we should not ~~~~~. We must be careful when ~~~~~. We should only ~~~~~.

Second, we should always ~~~~~. Lastly, once food has entered our mouth, we should not ~~~~~ until ~~~~~. ~~~~~ during meals. But we must remember to chew and swallow the food in our mouth ~~~~~. If we have to ~~~~~ in our mouth, we should always ~~~~~.

1 According to the passage, what must we do when speaking with food in our mouth?

(A) We should talk freely.
(B) We should cover our mouth.
(C) We should eat quietly.
(D) We should swallow the food.

2 In what order does the speaker talk about eating quietly?

(A) From putting food in our mouth to swallowing
(B) From talking to chewing quietly
(C) From breakfast to dinner
(D) From Western to Eastern culture

Listening Practice 2

Listen and choose the correct answer. As you listen, try to catch the hidden information.

Are the streets ~~_____~~ ? The problem is ~~_____~~ . People throw their ~~_____~~ . Littering is ~~_____~~ in many places. ~~_____~~ is to catch them and ~~_____~~ . ~~_____~~ usually ~~_____~~ , but we need ~~_____~~ to catch them. Another way to stop littering is ~~_____~~ on the streets. Most people are not bad people. They are ~~_____~~ . They don't want ~~_____~~ .

1 What is the talk mainly about?

(A) Bad litter
(B) Ways to stop littering
(C) More trash cans in neighborhoods
(D) Rubbish thrown by bad people

2 How does the speaker talk of solving the problem?

(A) He suggests ways to solve the problem.
(B) He talks about why trash is bad.
(C) He gives examples of what can happen.
(D) He compares clean and dirty streets.

Listening Practice 3

Listen and choose the correct answer.

memo

1 What is the talk mainly about?

(A) Gentle bullies
(B) Punishing bullies
(C) Ways to stop a bully
(D) Disturbing teachers

2 How does the teacher explain about bullies?

(A) By not telling the teachers
(B) By talking about how bullies study
(C) By contrasting fights with bullies
(D) By giving examples of what students can do

Listening Practice 4

Listen and choose the correct answer.

1 According to the speaker, what should we do when talking over the phone in public places?

(A) We should pay money to use the phone.
(B) We should talk very loudly on the phone.
(C) We should let the phone ring until it stops.
(D) We should talk quietly.

2 How does the speaker talk about manners?

(A) He gives examples of good manners.
(B) He compares rude people to himself.
(C) He talks about his personal experience.
(D) He talks about using public phones.

iBT Practice 1

TOEFL Listening

1 According to the teacher, what can exercise do for our minds?

    Ⓐ It will make us feel tired.
    Ⓑ It will make us feel fresh.
    Ⓒ It will exercise our brain.
    Ⓓ It will make us feel bad.

2 In what order does the teacher tell us about the good points of exercising?

    Ⓐ She talks of the muscles and then exercising.
    Ⓑ She talks of the lungs and then the heart.
    Ⓒ She talks of the body and then the mind.
    Ⓓ She talks of sitting down and then being lazy.

3 What is the talk mainly about?

    Ⓐ Walking at home
    Ⓑ Understanding traffic lights
    Ⓒ Walking on the street
    Ⓓ Driving on the road

4 How does the speaker talk about safety when walking on the street?

    Ⓐ He lists many ways to be safe.
    Ⓑ He talks about how the streets are dangerous.
    Ⓒ He talks of running on the walkway.
    Ⓓ He says roads are safe.

iBT Practice 2

TOEFL Listening

1 According to the speaker, why is it difficult to prepare for college?

- Ⓐ It is expensive.
- Ⓑ It takes a lot of work.
- Ⓒ It takes too much time.
- Ⓓ It makes you unhappy.

2 How does the speaker tell us that college is important?

- Ⓐ By saying that college is not a job
- Ⓑ By comparing college to school
- Ⓒ By giving examples of people in college
- Ⓓ By mentioning how college can help us

3 What is the conversation mainly about?

- Ⓐ Reasons to separate and recycle rubbish
- Ⓑ Separating rubbish to save energy
- Ⓒ Difficulty of separating rubbish
- Ⓓ Recyclable materials

4 How does the woman tell the man about the importance of recycling?

- Ⓐ She gives examples of recycling factories.
- Ⓑ She compares recycling and rubbish.
- Ⓒ She gives reasons why recycling is important.
- Ⓓ She talks of the importance of rubbish.

Dictation

iBT Practice 1 1-2

Listen and fill in the blanks. 43

Do you exercise often? Sometimes we _____ _____ _____ like exercising, but we must not be lazy _____ _____ _____. There are many reasons to exercise.

Exercising _____ our body _____. When we exercise, many muscles in our body move _____ _____ _____. Inner muscles, such as the heart and lungs, also need exercise. It is very important to exercise the heart to stay healthy _____ _____ _____ _____.

Exercising will also make _____ _____ fresh. Scientists proved that exercising and a healthy mind _____ _____. People _____ _____ _____ will not feel tired easily when studying and sitting down for a long time. They will feel good _____ _____.

iBT Practice 1 3-4

Listen and fill in the blanks.

_____ _____ _____ walk on the streets.

When we walk outside, we must be careful _____ _____

_____ _____.

　　We must always walk _____ _____ _____.

It is dangerous for people to walk on the road where the cars _____

_____ _____. There are many others who walk on the

walkway, so we should not suddenly stop _____ _____.

　　We _____ _____ _____ the road on the

crosswalk. _____ _____ the light is green, we should still

look left and right to check for cars. Once we are on the crossing, we should walk quickly

_____ _____ _____ _____.

iBT Practice 2 1-2

Listen and fill in the blanks. 🎧 45

    Going to college is an important event. _____ _____ _____ is not easy. You have to study a lot _____ _____ _____ _____.

Today, children _____ _____ for college. They have to get _____ _____. Why is going to college important?

    You need to go to college _____ _____ about the world. You also meet many people and learn to socialize better. College prepares you _____ _____ _____.

    Some people want to go to college _____ _____ _____ _____ that they want to do. If you don't go to college, getting a job will be difficult. _____ _____, do you want to become a doctor, a teacher _____ _____ _____? Then you need to study very hard.

iBT Practice 2 3-4

Listen and fill in the blanks. MP3 46

M: I hate _____ _____ like this. It's hard work.

W: It's not _____ _____ _____, but it is important for everyone. We are helping the world waste less and save energy.

M: Think about the energy to recycle. I think the energy _____ _____ _____ a new product or for recycling would be the same.

W: No, that is not true. Recycling factories use _____ _____ _____. They also do not use _____ _____ to make new products.

M: Alright, I understand that now, but I want to know _____ _____ _____ _____.

W: Because there are different recycling factories for different materials. It saves a lot of time for everyone _____ _____ _____ _____ now.

Word Review

Match the words from the box with the definitions.

| digestion | rubbish | swallow | litter |
| mean | disturb | punish | socialize |

1. _____ the process of changing food into the substances that your body needs

2. _____ food, paper, etc. that is no longer needed and has been thrown away

3. _____ to make food or drink go down your throat towards your stomach

4. _____ to leave waste paper, cans, etc. on the ground in a public place

5. _____ cruel or not kind

6. _____ to interrupt someone so that they cannot continue what they are doing

7. _____ to make someone suffer because they have done something wrong

8. _____ to interact with other people

Choose the best phrase to fit in each one of the blanks.

| switch off | at a time | such as | in trouble |

9. It is hard to think about more than one thing _____.

10. Be sure to _____ the lights when you leave the office at night.

11. He was _____ with the police because he broke the law.

12. College majors _____ engineering or physics can be very difficult.

Culture Corner

A: The radio said there will be a snowstorm tomorrow.
B: Good. Let's hope it will be terrible. That way, schools might close, and we can have a holiday.
A: Let's keep our fingers crossed.

Chapter 4
Technology

L.i.n.g.u.a.f.o.r.u.m. e-L.i.s.t.e.n.i.n.g

Chapter 4

Topic: Technology

Question Type:

Content-Identifying Relationship Questions

내용 관계 확인 문제

언급된 사항들간의 관계를 파악하는 문제

Content-Identifying Relationship Questions

내용 관계 확인 문제

○ 본과에서는 '내용 관계 확인(Content-Identifying Relationship)' 문제를 다룬다. 내용 관계 확인 문제란 들려 주는 글의 내용 속에서 분명하게 언급된(clearly stated) 사항들간의 관계를 확인하는 유형의 문제이다. 예를 들어, 글의 내용에서 언급된 사실이 무엇으로 비교가 되었는지 등에 대해 물어 볼 수 있다.

○ Content-Identifying Relationship을 묻는 유형의 질문은 주로 다음과 같다.

- What comparison is made between the two cameras?

Sample Question

TOEFL Listening

What comparison does the teacher make between steel and brick?

Ⓐ Cost and bricks
Ⓑ Design and stones
Ⓒ Houses and buildings
Ⓓ Strength and weight

Script & 해석

T: Humans used stones to make houses and buildings since a long time ago.
W: Do people still use stones to make houses?
T: Of course. Bricks are stones too. Then we discovered steel. Steel is used to make very tall buildings.
W: Why can't we use stones for tall buildings?
T: Because steel is much lighter and stronger than stone. Tall buildings are very heavy and need a lot of strength to support them.

T: 인간은 오래 전부터 집과 건물을 짓는데 돌을 이용해왔어.
W: 사람들이 아직도 집을 짓는데 돌을 이용하나요?
T: 물론이지. 벽돌도 돌이잖아. 그 후에 강철을 발견했어. 강철은 아주 높은 건물을 짓는데 이용되지.
W: 왜 높은 건물에는 돌을 사용할 수 없는 거지요?
T: 왜냐면 강철은 돌보다 훨씬 가볍고 강하거든. 높은 건물은 아주 무거운데 스스로를 지탱하려면 많은 힘이 필요해.

Basic Drills 1

Listen and choose the correct answer. MP3 48-50

1 They compare size between _____.

(A) 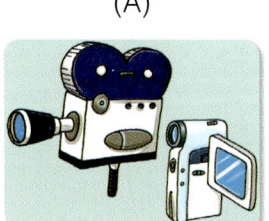 (B)  (C)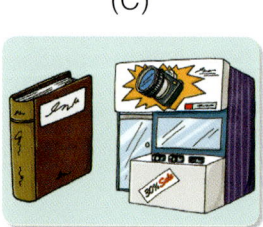

2 The speaker compares convenience between _____.

(A)  (B)  (C)

3 The speaker talks about speed between _____.

(A) 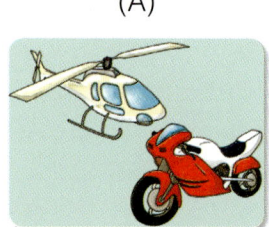 (B)  (C)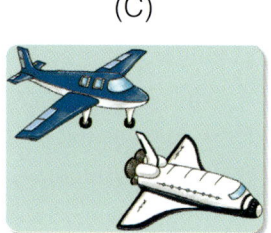

Basic Drills 2

Listen and choose the correct answer. MP3 51-53

1

What comparison is made between old and new cars?

(A) Safety
(B) Design

2

What comparison is made between the motorboats and sailboats?

(A) How they are made
(B) How they are pushed

3

What comparison is made between old and new phones?

(A) The size and weight of the phones
(B) The color of the phones

Listening Practice 1

Listen and choose the correct answer. As you listen, try to catch the hidden information.

In 1966, Ralph Baer made ~~~~~~~~~ called Pong. It was ~~~~~~~~~. Modern games are ~~~~~~~~~ Pong because they are ~~~~~~~. Why are modern video games this way?

One reason is because people want ~~~~~~~~~~~~~~~~. Real-looking games mean that players need to ~~~~~~ and ~~~~~~~~~. Older video games ~~~~~~~~~ because the games were ~~~~~ and ~~~~~.

Another reason is because ~~~~~~~~~~~~~~~~~. Game makers need ~~~~~~~~~ to make better games. This is why machines are very powerful.

1 What do players want in new video games?

(A) They want older games.
(B) They want easy games.
(C) They want more real-looking games.
(D) They want powerful games.

2 What comparison is made between new and old games?

(A) How long it takes to finish the games
(B) How expensive the games are
(C) How hard it is to make the games
(D) How many players can play the games

Listening Practice 2

Listen and choose the correct answer. As you listen, try to catch the hidden information.

M: I need to ~~~~~~~~~~.

W: ~~~~~~~~~~ are you going to buy?

M: I am still trying to decide between ~~~~~~~~~~ and ~~~~~~. I can't seem to ~~~~~~~~ ~~~~~~.

W: Yes, you are right. It is ~~~~~~~~ to make. AMD ~~~~~~~~~~~~ when it comes to games. Pentium is ~~~~~~~~~~, but ~~~~~~~~~~~~.

M: Well, I do ~~~~~~~~~~, but the computer will be ~~~~~~~~~~~~. Maybe ~~~~~~~~~ for me, but it is ~~~~~~~~~~. Oh, I don't know what I should do.

1 What is the conversation mainly about?

(A) Differences between AMD and Pentium
(B) Similarities between AMD and Pentium
(C) Computer games
(D) Computer programs

2 What comparison does the man make between Pentium and AMD?

(A) Speed of the internet
(B) Video and chatting
(C) Speed and price of the computers
(D) Popularity of the computers

Listening Practice 3

Listen and choose the correct answer.

MP3 56

memo

1 According to the speaker, what did radio stars do?

(A) They read the script with emotion.
(B) They read the script without emotion
(C) They made background effects.
(D) They saw drama in their heads.

2 What comparison is made between radio and television?

(A) The number of stars
(B) The number of channels
(C) The number of families
(D) The number of shows

Listening Practice 4

Listen and choose the correct answer.

memo

1 What is the conversation mainly about?

(A) Cell phones and public phones
(B) Good and bad points of a cell phone
(C) Many public phones on the street
(D) Being late to meet someone

2 What comparison does the woman make about the days before cell phones?

(A) Better life without cell phones
(B) Hard life without cell phones
(C) Number of public phones
(D) Number of emergencies

iBT Practice 1

TOEFL Listening

1 What comparison is made between old and new computers?

   Ⓐ Design and weight
   Ⓑ Speed and size
   Ⓒ Ease of use
   Ⓓ Computer rooms

2 Accordng to the man, what is a microchip?

   Ⓐ A It is a machine.
   Ⓑ It is the Nobel Prize.
   Ⓒ It is a brain for machines.
   Ⓓ It is a computer.

3 According to the conversation, how small can microchips be?

   Ⓐ As small as a dot
   Ⓑ Larger than a dot
   Ⓒ About the size of any machine
   Ⓓ Larger than a computer

4 What is the conversation mainly about?

- Ⓐ Using the internet to save lives
- Ⓑ Using the internet to send emails
- Ⓒ Using the internet to travel the world
- Ⓓ Using the internet to play games

5 What is the difference between normal and robot operations?

- Ⓐ The robot makes many mistakes.
- Ⓑ The operations are different and robots are dangerous.
- Ⓒ They are the same, but without the doctor.
- Ⓓ It is safer for robots to do the operation.

6 How can a robot perform the surgery?

- Ⓐ Doctors are controlled by the robot.
- Ⓑ The robot does the surgery by itself.
- Ⓒ The robot shares information online.
- Ⓓ A doctor controls the robot using special sticks.

iBT Practice 2

1 According to the student, what do digital cameras need?

    Ⓐ The internet
    Ⓑ Rolls of film
    Ⓒ A computer
    Ⓓ Older cameras

2 How does the student talk about digital cameras?

    Ⓐ She compares the design of cameras.
    Ⓑ She lists the benefits of digital cameras.
    Ⓒ She talks about the benefits of film cameras.
    Ⓓ She gives examples of digital cameras.

3 What comparison is made between the two cameras?

    Ⓐ The size of the cameras
    Ⓑ Their picture quality
    Ⓒ Computers and video cameras
    Ⓓ Storing pictures

4 What is the talk mainly about?

    Ⓐ The oldest car
    Ⓑ The fastest car
    Ⓒ The most expensive car
    Ⓓ The cheapest car

5 What comparison is made between the F1 and other cars?

    Ⓐ The speed of the car
    Ⓑ The size of the car
    Ⓒ The price of the car
    Ⓓ The looks of the car

6 How does the teacher say that the F1 is the best sports car in the world?

    Ⓐ She compares the F1 to big cars.
    Ⓑ She gives examples of good-looking cars.
    Ⓒ She gives reasons why it is the best.
    Ⓓ She lists other cars from Britain.

Dictation

Listen and fill in the blanks.

W: It's amazing _____ _____ is electronic.

M: Yes, because of the "microchip," things are _____ _____ now, and computers are quicker. Computers _____ _____ _____ slow and big.

W: What's a microchip?

M: It's _____ _____ for machines. Nearly every electronic machine has a microchip. It's a small but very important part of machines.

W: Just how small is it? And when _____ _____ _____?

M: Modern chips can be _____ _____ as a dot. They were first invented in 1959 _____ _____ _____ called "Texas Instruments." The inventor _____ a Nobel Prize.

W: I think he really _____ _____ _____. Without microchips, we would not have a lot of things _____ _____ every day.

*i*BT Practice **1** 4-6

Listen and fill in the blanks. MP3 59

W: What are _____ _____ of the internet?

M: I use it for email, playing games, _____ _____ with friends.

W: Do you know that the internet saves lives in hospitals too?

M: How is that possible? _____ _____ _____ that doctors share information online?

W: That is _____ _____. Also, doctors in another country can operate on patients _____ _____ _____.
A doctor on the other side of the world can control a robot _____ _____ _____.

M: Are you serious? The robot actually _____ _____ _____? That sounds dangerous. _____ _____ something goes wrong?

W: They have tested it for many years now _____ _____ _____ _____ safe. They only use it for emergencies if the patient needs the operation quickly. They say it is _____ _____ _____, but without the doctor.

iBT Practice 2 1-3

Listen and fill in the blanks. MP3 60

The first photograph _____ _____ in 1837. Digital cameras were invented _____ _____ by Kodak. We can also find cameras in our cell phones. Cameras are now part _____ _____ _____.

Digital cameras can store many pictures _____ _____. Users can choose to take many pictures, and only keep the pictures _____ _____ _____. Older cameras did not store pictures; they used film. The number of pictures _____ _____ what kind of film the user had.

Digital cameras are cheap _____ _____. They have no film to buy and develop like older cameras. Digital cameras only need a computer _____ _____ the pictures. This makes it cheap and easy for people _____ _____ their pictures and video on the internet.

iBT Practice 2 4-6

Listen and fill in the blanks. MP3 61

_____ _____ like big cars. _____ like good-looking cars. Many people love really fast sports cars. Do you know what is the fastest sports car in the world?

   The McLaren F1 _____ _____ is the fastest sports car in the world. It was made in 1991. It can go _____ 400 kilometers per hour. Only 100 _____ _____. It took more than a year _____ _____ _____ _____. Even today, the F1 is the fastest car _____ _____ _____.

   Why is the car _____ _____? The engine is very powerful, and the car is _____ _____. The shape of the car _____ _____ _____ to go very quickly. This is why the car is so fast.

Word Review

Match the words from the box with the definitions.

| erase | emotion | imagination | invent |
| deserve | maintain | surgery | weapon |

1 _____ to make something stay the same

2 _____ the ability to form pictures or ideas in your mind

3 _____ to remove or get rid of something completely

4 _____ medical treatment in which a doctor cuts open your body

5 _____ to have a right to something because of the way you have behaved

6 _____ to design or create something that did not exist before

7 _____ a feeling that you experience such as love, anger, or fear

8 _____ something that you use to kill or hurt people in a fight or a war, such as a gun, knife, or bomb

Choose the best phrase to fit in each one of the blanks.

| provided ... with ... | made up her mind | depend on | between ... and ... |

9 The school _____ the teacher _____ housing and salary.

10 People _____ computers for many things in everyday life.

11 She found it hard to choose _____ history _____ math for her college major.

12 Cathy _____ to lose weight, and then did so.

Culture Corner

Throwing a coin in a fountain

A: Look, there's a fountain.
B: Give me a coin quickly. I want to make a wish.
A: Sorry, I only have one coin, and I need to make a wish myself.

•• People long ago believed that the sea gods controlled the water, so they threw money in the wells. We know this is not true, but people still throw coins in fountains and make a wish.

Chapter 5
History

Chapter 5

Topic:

History

Question Type:

Stance /Attitude Questions

입장/태도 문제

화자의 태도를 파악하는 문제

Stance/Attitude Questions
입장/태도 문제

○ 본과에서는 '입장/태도(Stance/Attitude)' 문제를 다룬다. 입장/태도 문제란 주어진 사실에 대해 화자가 어떠한 태도(attitude)를 취하는지, 또는 화자가 그 사실에 대해 말할 때 어느 정도의 확실한 입장(stance)을 취하고 있는지에 대한 이해를 확인하는 문제이다.
  • Stance/Attitude 문제에서는 🎧 표시가 나오면서 들려준 글의 내용 중에서 특정 부분을 한번 더 들려주고 그 부분에 대한 질문을 한다.

○ Stance/Attitude에 대해 묻는 유형의 질문은 다음과 같다.

> • What is the student's attitude toward the people?
> • What does the man mean when he says this: 🎧

Sample Question

TOEFL Listening

Listen again to part of the talk. Then answer the question.
What does the teacher mean when he says this:

Ⓐ He is not sure of the answer.
Ⓑ He expects the students to ask.
Ⓒ He wants to talk more about it.
Ⓓ He wants to compare with other buildings.

Script & 해석

I believe all of you have heard of the "Taj Mahal." The Taj Mahal is located in Agra, India. It is one of the most beautiful buildings in the world. The Taj Mahal looks beautiful in any weather. The King made the designer blind after it was finished to make sure that he could not build another one. So what is the Taj Mahal? **Why is the Taj Mahal so special?** The Taj Mahal is the grave for the Indian Queen, Mumtaz Mahal. The King loved the Queen very much, and was very sad when she died. The King ordered the people to build the Taj Mahal to remember the Queen.

여러분은 모두 타지 마할에 대해 들어봤을 것이다. 타지 마할은 인도 아그라에 있다. 그것은 세상에서 가장 아름다운 건축물 중 하나이다. 그 건축물은 어떤 날씨에서도 아름다워 보인다. 왕은 건축가가 그 이후 다른 건물을 만들지 못하게 하기 위해 건물을 지은 직후 건축가의 눈을 멀게 했다. 그럼 타지 마할은 무엇일까? 타지 마할은 왜 그렇게 특별한 것일까? 타지 마할은 인도의 왕비 뭄타즈 마할의 무덤이다. 왕은 여왕을 너무 사랑했기 때문에 그녀가 죽자 매우 슬펐다. 왕은 왕비를 기억하기 위해 사람들을 시켜 타지 마할을 짓도록 명령했다.

Basic Drills 1

Listen and choose the correct answer. MP3 63-65

1 What did the two people think about the TV show?

(A)    (B) 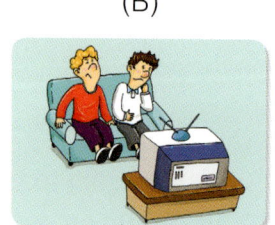   (C)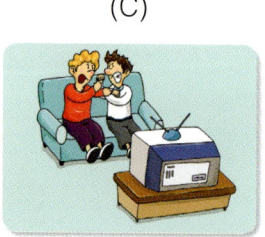

2 What are the two people feeling?

(A)    (B)    (C)

3 How is the man feeling?

(A) 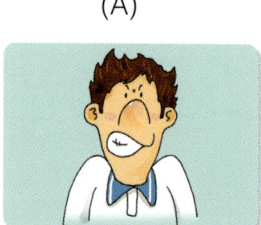   (B) 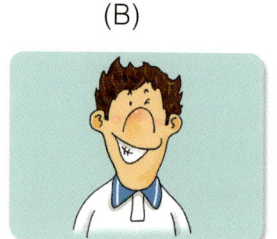   (C)

Basic Drills 2

Listen and choose the correct answer. MP3 66-68

1

Does the man believe in Bigfoot?

(A) He does believe.

(B) He does not believe.

2

Can scientists fully understand the picture language?

(A) Yes, they can fully understand the language.

(B) No, they only understand a little.

3

Do scientists know why ships and planes disappear?

(A) No, they are not sure.

(B) Yes, they are sure.

Listening Practice 1

Listen and choose the correct answer. As you listen, try to catch the hidden information.

I'd like to talk about ~~~~~~~~~~. I was ~~~~~~ about the news, just like everyone else. Many countries were hit, but ~~~~~~~~~~.

~~~~~~~~~~~~~ by the tsunami. When the tsunami started there, at least ~~~~~~~. Whole towns ~~~~~~~. The waves came into the towns and ~~~~~~~, including the trees and roads. ~~~~~~~~~ by the tsunami. ~~~~~~~ in the tsunami. Even ~~~~~~~~ changed. Nothing could survive the giant deadly waves.

1 According to the passage, where did the tsunami start?

(A) In Sri Lanka
(B) In a foreign country
(C) In Indonesia
(D) In Europe

2 What does the speaker mean when he says this: 🎧

(A) He thinks that only he was shocked.
(B) He knows that everyone was shocked as he was.
(C) He thinks that some were surprised.
(D) He knows that nobody was surprised.

Listening Practice 2

Listen and choose the correct answer. As you listen, try to catch the hidden information.

W: What do you know about ⬚⬚⬚ ?

M: I heard that ⬚⬚⬚ as a present.

W: That's good. Did you also know that ⬚⬚⬚ ?

M: Excuse me? It looks ⬚⬚⬚ that I see.

W: The French used ⬚⬚⬚ . Copper is a type of metal. ⬚⬚⬚ .

M: So when did the statue ⬚⬚⬚ ?

W: When the statue ⬚⬚⬚ , it was very dark brown. ⬚⬚⬚ , the statue turned into ⬚⬚⬚ .

1 What is the conversation mainly about?

(A) The color of the of the statue
(B) The size of the statue
(C) The meaning of the statue
(D) The location of the statue

2 Listen again to part of the conversation. Then answer the question. What does the student mean when he says this: 🎧

(A) He thought the pictures were green.
(B) He thought the statue was always green.
(C) He knew the statue was a different color.
(D) He knew the statue was not green.

Listening Practice 3

Listen and choose the correct answer.

MP3 71

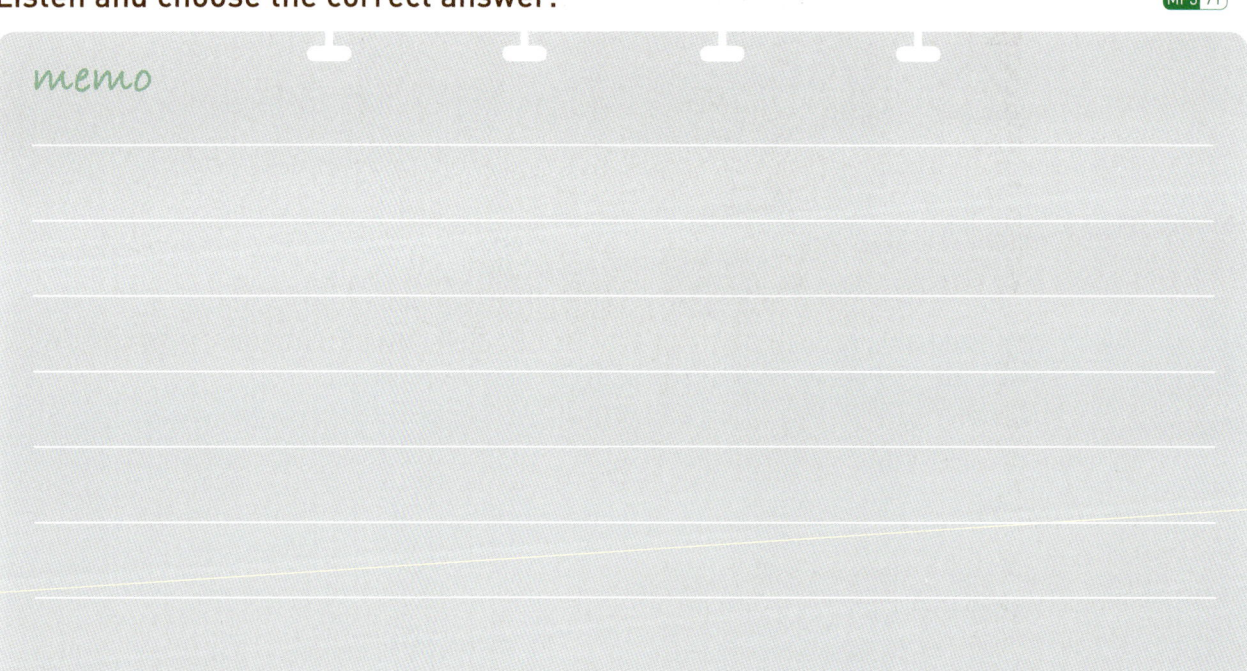
memo

1 Listen again to part of the discussion. Then answer the question.
What does the student mean when he says this: 🎧

(A) He does not know who won.
(B) He is not surprised that the Americans lost.
(C) He is surprised that the Russians won.
(D) He believes that America won.

2 What is the discussion mainly about?

(A) Spaceships of the Russians and the Americans
(B) Space race between the Russians and the Americans
(C) Marathon race between the Russians and the Americans
(D) Race to build a spaceship

96 e-Listening

Listening Practice 4

Listen and choose the correct answer.

memo

1 What is implied about sailing around South America before the canal?

(A) People enjoyed sailing around South America.
(B) It was dangerous for ships.
(C) It was safe for ships.
(D) Ships saved a lot of time.

2 What is the main topic of the talk?

(A) Building the Panama Canal
(B) When the Panama Canal was built
(C) Pirates of the Panama Canal
(D) The benefits of the Panama Canal

iBT Practice 1

TOEFL Listening

1 What happened when the two sides joined?

  A There are still two Germanys.
  B It was not big news.
  C The West had to use a lot of money.
  D The East had to use a lot of money.

2 What comparison is made between East and West Germany?

  A People
  B Weather
  C Economy
  D Houses

3 Listen again to part of the conversation. Then answer the question. What does the man mean when he says this:

  A He implies that he lived in Berlin.
  B He implies that he does not know about it.
  C He implies that he knows a lot.
  D He implies that he has been to the Berlin.

4 What is the talk mainly about?

- Ⓐ Understanding the pyramids
- Ⓑ Designing the pyramids
- Ⓒ Building the pyramids
- Ⓓ Burial in the pyramids

5 What did grave robbers want from the pyramids?

- Ⓐ They wanted the Pharaoh's gold.
- Ⓑ They wanted the Pharaoh's writing.
- Ⓒ They wanted the Pharaoh's servants.
- Ⓓ They wanted the servants' gold.

6 Listen again to part of the talk. Then answer the question.
What does the teacher mean when he says this:

- Ⓐ He implies that pyramids have no meaning.
- Ⓑ He implies that we don't understand at all.
- Ⓒ He implies that we understand everything.
- Ⓓ He implies that we cannot know everything.

iBT Practice 2

TOEFL Listening

1. What is the talk mainly about?

   Ⓐ The color of the Great Wall
   Ⓑ The building of the Great Wall
   Ⓒ The people that made the Great Wall
   Ⓓ The materials used on the Great Wall

2. According to the teacher, how long was the original wall?

   Ⓐ 6,400 kilometers
   Ⓑ 5,000 kilometers
   Ⓒ 50,000 kilometers
   Ⓓ 2,000 kilometers

3. Listen again to part of the talk. Then answer the question.
   What does the teacher mean when she says this:

   Ⓐ She thinks it was hard to build the wall long ago.
   Ⓑ She thinks 2,000 years is short.
   Ⓒ She thinks it's easy to build walls.
   Ⓓ She thinks the wall is short.

4 What is the conversation mainly about?

- Ⓐ World War I
- Ⓑ World War II
- Ⓒ Controlling another country
- Ⓓ Nazis and Hitler

5 According to the conversation, who wanted more power?

- Ⓐ Germany and Japan
- Ⓑ US and other countries
- Ⓒ Korea and China
- Ⓓ The whole world

6 Listen again to part of the conversation. Then answer the question. What does the man mean when he says this:

- Ⓐ He is surprised that few people died.
- Ⓑ He does not know that people died.
- Ⓒ He thinks that nobody died.
- Ⓓ He is sad that many people died.

Dictation

iBT Practice 1 1-3

Listen and fill in the blanks.

W: Do you _____ _____ about the Berlin Wall?

M: Excuse me?

W: The Berlin Wall.

M: I only know it was in Berlin.

W: That wall _____ _____ _____ East and West Germany. The Berlin Wall _____ _____ in 1989.

M: Wow. Many people must have been interested in it.

W: Yes, it was very big news. East Germany was very poor. _____ _____ was very bad. They were not like West Germany.

M: What do you mean, not like West Germany?

W: West Germany's economy was _____ _____ _____ _____ _____. The whole world liked West German products.

M: So what happened _____ _____ _____?

W: A lot of people were afraid that Germany would face problems. West Germany had to use a lot of money _____ _____ the two economies. But at the end, they were successful, and now there is only one Germany.

iBT Practice 1 4-6

Listen and fill in the blanks. MP3 74

The most _____ _____ _____ are in Egypt. The pyramids were _____ _____ of Pharaohs. There are many things we do not understand about the pyramids, but we can find some answers _____ _____ the writings on the pyramids.

The pyramids are very hard _____ _____. They are _____ _____. Some pyramids still have rooms _____ _____ _____. The pyramids were designed this way because of grave robbers. Grave robbers stole the Pharaohs' gold and other things _____ _____ _____ _____.

The pyramids also have _____ _____ _____. The old Egyptians believed that the Pharaohs needed servants after they _____ _____, so they killed the Pharaohs' servants and buried them together in the pyramid.

iBT Practice 2 1-3

Listen and fill in the blanks. MP3 75

    The Great Wall of China is _____ _____ that we can see it _____ _____. It is the biggest thing _____ _____ _____. It is very long and tall. It is amazing to think that the wall was made over 2,000 years ago.

    The walls _____ _____ by the First Emperor of China _____ _____ _____ _____ the Mongols. _____ _____ _____ was about 5,000 kilometers.

    More walls were built during the Han dynasty. _____ _____, the walls had weapons and guard towers to fight _____ _____ _____.

iBT Practice 2 4-6

Listen and fill in the blanks. MP3 76

M: What _____ _____ _____ about World War II?

W: I heard that Germany and Japan were part of the war.

M: Yes, but other countries were _____ _____ _____ _____ _____. Germany and Japan were trying to have more power _____ _____ other countries.

W: Are you talking about Hitler?

M: Yes, he was a Nazi. The Nazis _____ they were better _____ _____, and killed a lot of people.

W: How about Japan? They fought with a lot of countries too.

M: Japan took over many countries, _____ Korea, China and other countries. They hurt people _____ _____ _____ to learn about Japan. They also attacked the US.

W: So how did the war end?

M: Germany finally _____ _____ _____, and Americans dropped _____ _____ _____ in Japan. A total of 60 million people died in the war. Too many people died.

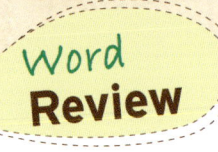

Word Review

Match the words from the box with the definitions.

| ancient | compass | survive | pirate |
| divide | royal | maze | servant |

1 _____ to separate people or things into smaller groups or parts

2 _____ someone who is hired to work for another, especially in the household

3 _____ relating to a king or queen

4 _____ an instrument that shows directions and has a needle that always points north

5 _____ a complex system of paths which is difficult to find the way through

6 _____ relating to a time long ago in history, especially thousands of years ago

7 _____ to continue to live in spite of many problems or difficulties

8 _____ someone who attacks other ships and steals things from them

Choose the best phrase to fit in each one of the blanks.

| is located in | is well known for | used to | washed away |

9 The island _____ for its beautiful beaches and white sands.

10 We _____ go fishing at the river when we were young.

11 The flood _____ several houses, but no one was injured.

12 The hotel _____ the center of the city and is easy to reach by public transportation.

106 e-Listening

Culture Corner

Potluck Party

A: Hey, what are you taking to Susan's potluck party?
B: I was thinking about a roast. It's my specialty.
A: Oh, good! I tried it in my potluck party.
   It was delicious!

•• Many parties overseas are potluck parties. This means that the guests must bring one type of food to the event. Potluck parties are popular in areas with different cultural backgrounds.

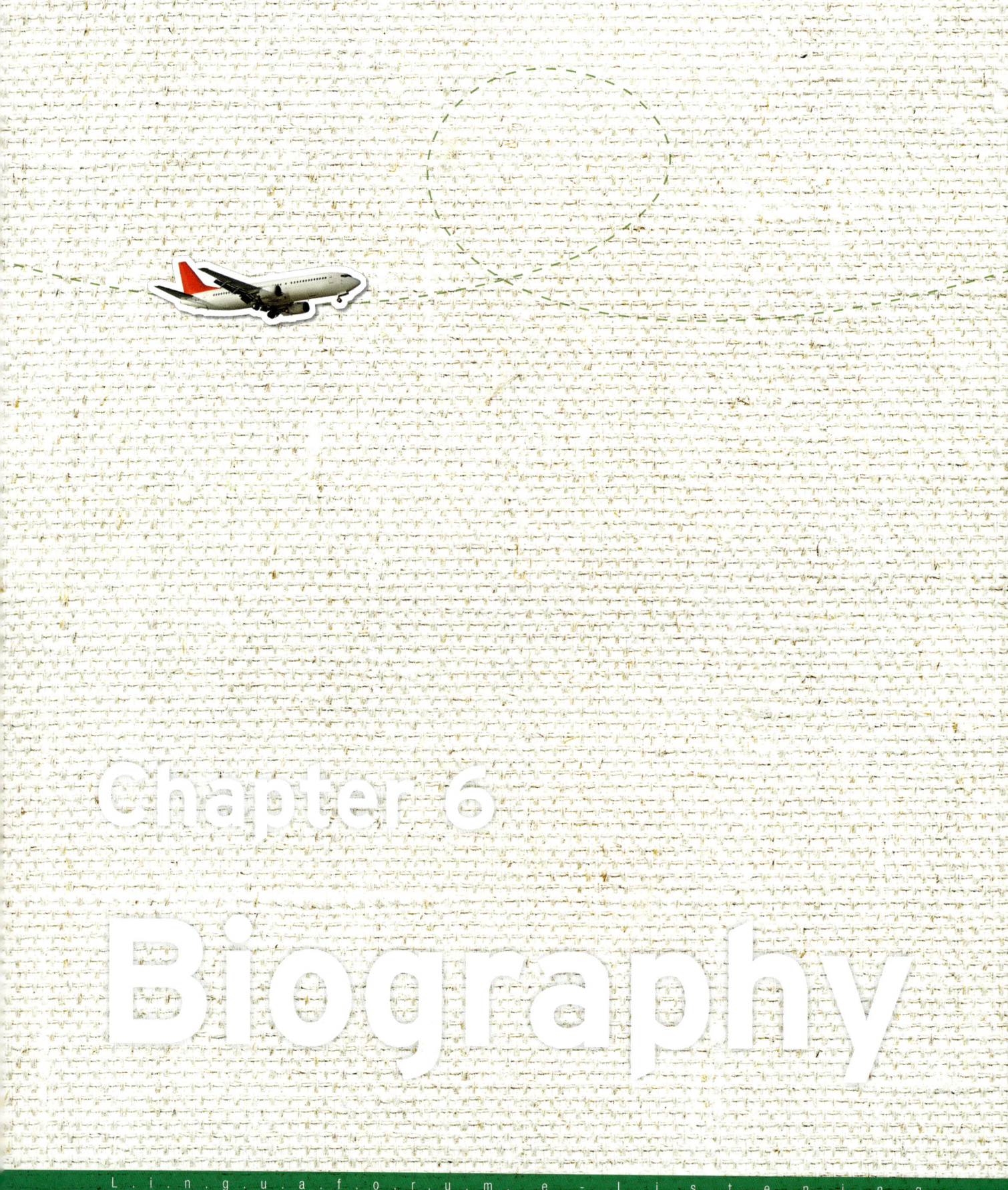

Chapter 6
Biography

Chapter 6

Topic:
Biography

Question Type:
Function-Purpose Questions
표현 목적 파악 문제
화자가 말한 내용의 의도를 파악하는 문제

Function-Purpose Questions
표현 목적 파악 문제

○ 본과에서는 '표현 목적 파악(Function-Purpose)' 문제를 다룬다. 표현 목적 파악 문제란 화자(speaker)가 말한 특정 표현의 궁극적인 의도나 의미를 글의 맥락 속에서 파악하는 능력을 묻는 문제이다. 예를 들어, "Excuse me."라는 표현이 사과의 의미로 사용이 되었는지, 상대방의 주의를 환기시키기 위한 의도로 한 말인지를 물어 볼 수 있다. Stance/Attitude 문제에서와 같이 🎧 표시가 나오면서 특정 표현을 재생(replay)하여 들려주고 그 부분의 의미 또는 말한 의도에 대해 질문을 한다.

○ Function-Purpose를 묻는 질문의 유형은 다음과 같다.

> • Why does the woman say this: 🎧

Sample Question

TOEFL Listening

Listen again to part of the talk. Then answer the question.
Why does the teacher say this:

Ⓐ To compare other names for Michael
Ⓑ To express how famous Michael is
Ⓒ To encourage Michael's popularity
Ⓓ To give an example of a king

Script & 해석

There are many famous people in music, but Michael Jackson might be the most famous musician of them all. Michael Jackson has been a singer since he was very young. He and his brothers had a successful band called "The Jackson 5." Michael was the lead singer of the group. When Michael grew up, he started his own music. He had many hits and records under his name. He also made many new dance moves, such as the Moonwalk. There might never be another star as famous or popular as Michael Jackson. **It is no surprise that people call him the King of Pop.**

음악계에는 유명한 사람들이 많지만 마이클 잭슨은 아마 그들 중에 가장 유명한 사람일 것이다. 마이클 잭슨은 아주 어릴 적부터 가수였다. 그와 그의 형제들은 '잭슨 파이브'라고 하는 성공적인 밴드를 만들었다. 마이클 잭슨은 그룹의 리드싱어였다. 마이클은 성인이 되자 자신만의 음악을 시작한다. 그는 그의 이름으로 많은 히트곡과 음반을 냈다. 그는 문워크 같은 춤도 들었다. 마이클 잭슨처럼 유명하고 인기 있는 스타는 아마 결코 없을 것이다. 사람들이 그를 팝의 황제라고 부른 것은 너무 당연하다.

Basic Drills 1

Listen and choose the correct answer. MP3 78-80

1 Why does the woman say this: 🎧

(A) To say that she cannot hear the man
(B) To show that she is shocked
(C) To ask what operation he is having

2 Why does the man say this: 🎧

(A) To show that the woman is rude
(B) To show that he is sorry
(C) To say that he is also busy

3 Why does the woman say this: 🎧

(A) To say that she studied
(B) To agree with the man
(C) To show that she doesn't believe the man

Basic Drills 2

Listen and choose the correct answer. MP3 81-83

1

memo

Why does the speaker say this: 🎧

(A) To show Washington as a great leader
(B) To compare Washington to other leaders

2

memo

Why does the speaker mention other black leaders?

(A) To contrast who was a better leader
(B) To show that King was different

3

memo

Why does the speaker say this: 🎧

(A) To say that Napoleon made a mistake
(B) To stress that Napoleon won

Listening Practice 1

Listen and choose the correct answer. As you listen, try to catch the hidden information.

Abraham Lincoln is one of ~~_____~~ of America. He did ~~_____~~ ~~_____~~ in the United States. One of them was ~~_____~~. When Lincoln was president, there were many people ~~_____~~. Lincoln stopped ~~_____~~. The South was unhappy and ~~_____~~. The North and South had ~~_____~~. Lincoln ~~_____~~.

Lincoln ~~_____~~ while watching a play. A man ~~_____~~. Many people were sad ~~_____~~. Even today, people still remember Abraham Lincoln ~~_____~~.

1 What is the talk mainly about?

(A) The life of Abraham Lincoln
(B) Slaves in the North
(C) Slaves in the East
(D) War with the South

2 Why does the speaker say this: 🎧

(A) To stress that people do not remember Lincoln anymore
(B) To say that Lincoln was killed today
(C) To imply that people will remember Lincoln from today
(D) To stress that many still think that Lincoln was a great man

Listening Practice 2

MP3 85

Listen and choose the correct answer. As you listen, try to catch the hidden information.

W: I just ~~~~~~~~~~ .

M: Really? How was ~~~~~~ ?

W: It was great. I got to see ~~~~~~~~ .

M: That's wonderful! ~~~~~~~~~ ?

W: Oh yes, it was very beautiful. Did you know that ~~~~~~~~~~~~~~~~~~~~~ ?
People thought that the tower made up of ~~~~~~~~~~~ .

M: Yes, but ~~~~~~~~~ , people thought ~~~~~~~~ .

W: Yes. Oh, did you know that ~~~~~~~~~~~~~ , also helped build ~~~~~ ~~~~~~ ? Wasn't he ~~~~~~~~~ to do such things?

M: Wow, I didn't know that. I guess you learned a lot of things in Paris.

1 Listen again to part of the conversation. Then answer the question.
Why does the man say this: 🎧

(A) To show that she is beautiful
(B) To say that the tower is beautiful
(C) To show that he wants to know more
(D) To stress that the tower is beautiful

2 How does the woman emphasize Gustave Eiffel as a great man?

(A) By mentioning the tower's height
(B) By talking about Eiffel's work
(C) By comparing Eiffel to other builders
(D) By comparing him to the Eiffel Tower

Chapter 6. Biography 115

Listening Practice 3

Listen and choose the correct answer.

memo

1 Listen again to part of the talk. Then answer the question.
Why does the teacher say this: 🎧

(A) To know if the students follow Picasso
(B) To check if the students understand
(C) To finish the talk
(D) To begin talking about Picasso

2 When were Picasso's pictures more expensive?

(A) After Picasso died
(B) When da Vinci was alive
(C) When Picasso was alive
(D) When art was not popular

Listening Practice 4

Listen and choose the correct answer.

1 What is the conversation mainly about?

(A) Giving up everything
(B) Helping the poor
(C) The work of Mother Theresa
(D) The comfortable life of Mother Theresa

2 Listen again to part of the conversation. Then answer the question.
Why does the woman say this:

(A) To say that Mother Theresa didn't do a lot of things
(B) To agree that Mother Theresa was great
(C) To say that she thinks of Mother Theresa
(D) To say that she can do what Mother Theresa did

iBT Practice 1

TOEFL Listening

1. What are the things that Lance has done? Tick in the correct box.

	Yes	No
Ⓐ He raced bicycles.		
Ⓑ He fought cancer.		
Ⓒ He opened a hosptal.		
Ⓓ He retired from bicycle racing.		

2. Listen again to part of the talk. Then answer the question. Why does the teacher say this: 🎧

   Ⓐ To mention that Lance is also famous for other things
   Ⓑ To say that people only know him as a patient
   Ⓒ To say that he is not very famous
   Ⓓ To give examples of bicycle champions

3. Listen again to part of the talk. Then answer the question. Why does the teacher say this: 🎧

   Ⓐ To show that Lance likes to be a hero
   Ⓑ To state that Lance is a sick person
   Ⓒ To express that Lance is a special person
   Ⓓ To indicate that Lance is normal

4 What is the conversation mainly about?

    Ⓐ Light bulbs
    Ⓑ Inventions of inventors
    Ⓒ Inventions of Edison
    Ⓓ An electric company

5 According to the conversation, what is true about Thomas Edison? Tick in the correct box.

	Yes	No
Ⓐ Edison invented the light bulb.		
Ⓑ Edison invented the video camera.		
Ⓒ Edison invented the television.		
Ⓓ Edison invented electricity.		

6 Listen again to part of the conversation. Then answer the question. Why does the man say this: 🎧

    Ⓐ To find out if she knows more
    Ⓑ To try and see the list of inventions
    Ⓒ To ask her what she thinks of the inventions
    Ⓓ To try and remember some inventions

iBT Practice 2

TOEFL Listening

1. What is the conversation mainly about?

   A. Winners of the Nobel Prize
   B. How dynamites work
   C. Life of Alfred Nobel
   D. Dynamite companies

2. Listen again to part of the conversation. Then answer the question. Why does the man say this:

   A. To ask about Nobel
   B. To see if she knows about Nobel
   C. To stress that he does not know about Nobel
   D. To show his surprise that she doesn't know him

3. Listen again to part of the conversation. Then answer the question. Why does the woman say this:

   A. To show that she does not believe it
   B. To agree with the man
   C. To say that she does not know about it
   D. To show that she likes Nobel

4 According to the conversation, why was General Lee famous?

   Ⓐ He built a ship that beat the Japanese.
   Ⓑ He built a special ship for the Japanese.
   Ⓒ He sold the ship to the Japanese.
   Ⓓ He lost the war with the Japanese.

5 Listen again to part of the conversation. Then answer the question. Why does the woman say this: 🎧

   Ⓐ To express her happiness
   Ⓑ To express her disappointment
   Ⓒ To finish off the conversation
   Ⓓ To start another conversation

6 Listen again to part of the conversation. Then answer the question. Why does the man say this: 🎧

   Ⓐ To compare General Lee and a turtle
   Ⓑ To compare other ships during General Lee's time
   Ⓒ To give examples of what can happen to ships
   Ⓓ To express the importance of the ship

Dictation

iBT Practice 1 1-3

Listen and fill in the blanks. MP3 88

    The world's most important bicycle race is in France. The best bicycle riders from all over the world _____ _____ _____ _____. The best well-known champion is Lance Armstrong. He _____ _____ _____ many times. But Lance Armstrong is also known _____ _____ _____.

    Lance Armstrong had _____. Many doctors said that Lance could die. Lance did not give up _____ _____ _____ _____ the cancer. He _____ _____ a lot of hard treatment in hospital. It was very hard for Lance to fight, but he won. After that, he went to race. _____ _____, he has won six races.

    Lance also started an organization _____ the Armstrong Foundation. The group helps _____ _____ have a normal life. He is truly everyone's hero.

iBT Practice 1 4-6

Listen and fill in the blanks. MP3 89

M: Thomas Edison was _____ _____ _____.
   He invented so many things.

W: Isn't he _____ _____ _____? How many things did he invent?

M: I heard that Edison and his electric company invented _____ _____ 1,000 inventions when Edison was alive.

W: Wow. That is a lot. What _____ _____ _____ is his most important invention?

M: It has to be _____ _____ _____. Light bulbs are very important to us. We use them everywhere.

W: That is true. I wonder _____ _____ he invented that we use every day.

M: Let's see. There are _____ _____ _____.

W: I remember one. He invented _____ _____ _____. Without it, we would not have anything to watch on TV.

M: Yes, you're right. That was a very important invention, too.

Chapter 6. Biography 123

iBT Practice 2 1-3

Listen and fill in the blanks. MP3 90

W: Who is Nobel? I saw something _____ _____ last night.

M: _____ _____ _____ about Alfred Nobel?

W: No, I don't. Who was he?

M: He was a Swedish inventor _____ _____ _____. Many companies needed dynamite, and so he was very successful.

W: His family _____ _____ _____ very happy about it.

M: He did not marry, so he didn't have a wife _____ _____. He decided to use all the money _____ _____ _____ the Nobel Prize.

W: Yeah, right.

M: It's true. He was sad _____ _____ _____ that dynamite was also used to kill people. He wanted _____ _____ people who did great things for others.

iBT Practice 2 4-6

Listen and fill in the blanks. MP3 91

W: _____ _____ do you know about General Lee? They say he did many great things.

M: Oh yes, everyone knows General Lee.

W: Really? Tell me more _____ _____.

M: Well, he was _____ _____ of the Korean army a long time ago. He _____ a ship.

W: Is that all? Anyone can draw a ship.

M: Not just any ship. General Lee made _____ _____ _____ called the turtle ship. The outside was very strong, _____ _____ _____ _____ were safe. It was not like normal ships.

W: Now that you mention it, I do remember seeing a picture _____ _____ _____ _____. Does it have an angry turtle head on top of the ship?

M: Yes, those are the turtle ships. General Lee used the turtle ships _____ _____ _____ the Japanese. That is why he is so famous.

Word Review

Match the words from the box with the definitions.

| protest | respect | follower | general |
| enemy | slave | normal | reward |

1. _____ to make a return for something
2. _____ a strong public expression of disapproval or complaint
3. _____ someone who is owned by another and has no freedom
4. _____ an officer of a high rank in the army or air force
5. _____ usual; without any special characteristics
6. _____ to think highly of or have a good opinion of someone
7. _____ someone who supports a particular person, group, or belief
8. _____ someone who hates you and wants to harm you

Choose the best phrase to fit in each one of the blanks.

| grew up | in the end | give up | set up |

9. The child wanted to be a singer when she _____.

10. The newsboy _____ a stand and sold newspapers.

11. A number of women are still forced to _____ their jobs when they get married or have children.

12. The race was very close, but _____ our team won by 5 points.

126   e-Listening

Culture Corner

Knock on Wood

A: I'm going to ski down this hill.
B: It looks quite dangerous. Hope you don't hurt yourself. Knock on wood.
A: Thanks. I need all the luck I can get.

•• Long ago, people believed that spirits lived in trees. Americans often "touch" or "knock" on wood just before they do something that might need luck. This is why some places even have a piece of wood, so people can have luck.

Mini Test 1-3

Mini Test 1

TOEFL Listening

TOEFL Listening

1. What is the conversation mainly about?
   - Ⓐ Thinking about computer games
   - Ⓑ Going back in time
   - Ⓒ Forgetting about the test and playing games
   - Ⓓ A test on computer games

2. According to the conversation, what is the test about?
   - Ⓐ The history of Korea
   - Ⓑ A computer game
   - Ⓒ Taking notes
   - Ⓓ Korean games

3. Listen to part of the conversation. Then answer the question. What does the woman mean when she says this:
   - Ⓐ She wishes that she could go back home now.
   - Ⓑ She regrets that she did not study the night before.
   - Ⓒ She is confident that she will do well on the test.
   - Ⓓ She wants to study with him after school.

4. Listen to part of the conversation. Then answer the question. Why does the man say this:
   - Ⓐ To provide her with information for the test
   - Ⓑ To suggest playing computer games together
   - Ⓒ To pray that she would do well on the test
   - Ⓓ To tell her that it's too late to study for the test

Mini Test 1

5 What is the talk mainly about?

- Ⓐ Exciting fishing
- Ⓑ Swordfish's long nose
- Ⓒ Dangerous sea
- Ⓓ Dangers of long-line fishing

6 According to the student, what are the reasons long-line fishing is dangerous? Tick in the correct box.

	Yes	No
Ⓐ Fish close to land		
Ⓑ Dangerous swordfish		
Ⓒ Many other fishermen		
Ⓓ No safe place in the ocean		

7 Why does the speaker mention swordfish?

- Ⓐ To compare them to other fish
- Ⓑ To explain the physical characteristics of swordfish
- Ⓒ To tell about one of the dangers of long-line fishing
- Ⓓ To introduce the next topic of discussion

8 What is the speaker's attitude toward long-line fishing?

- Ⓐ It is fun.
- Ⓑ It is boring.
- Ⓒ It is expensive.
- Ⓓ It is not safe.

Mini Test 1

TOEFL Listening

9 What is the talk mainly about?

- A Selling a chocolate cake
- B Making a chocolate cake
- C Making a fruit cake
- D Eating a chocolate cake

10 In what order are cakes made?

- A Mix, bake, and decorate
- B Decorate and mix
- C Eat and decorate
- D Eat and bake

11 According to the talk, what are the steps to make a chocolate cake? Tick in the correct box.

	Yes	No
A Mix flour, eggs, milk and sugar together		
B Mix the dough into a pretty shape		
C Put inside a hot oven for 3 hours		
D Sprinkle chocolate flakes on the cake		

12 Listen again to part of the talk. Then answer the question. What does the speaker mean when she says this: 🎧

- A We cannot eat with our left hands.
- B The cake is still not finished.
- C We must eat on the left.
- D The cake is finished at this stage.

Mini Test 2

TOEFL Listening

TOEFL Listening

1 What is the conversation mainly about?

Ⓐ Mom and dad in pictures
Ⓑ Movies of the 60s
Ⓒ Short hairstyles in the 60s
Ⓓ Funny fashion of the 60s

2 What do they think of 60s fashion?

Ⓐ They want to do the same things.
Ⓑ They think it is fashionable.
Ⓒ They think it is funny.
Ⓓ They want to find more 60s fashion.

3 According to the conversation, who had short hair in the 60s?

Ⓐ Most people had short hair.
Ⓑ Not many people had short hair.
Ⓒ Everyone had short hair.
Ⓓ Nobody had short hair.

4 Listen again to part of the conversation. Then answer the question. What does the man mean when he says this: 🎧

Ⓐ He does not like the pants.
Ⓑ He is not talking about those pants.
Ⓒ He wants those pants.
Ⓓ He wants to see the pants.

Mini Test 2

5 What is the talk mainly about?

- Ⓐ The bad effects of computer games
- Ⓑ The development of computer games
- Ⓒ The educational use of computer games
- Ⓓ The growing popularity of computer games

6 What do new games have in common?

- Ⓐ They do not look real.
- Ⓑ They try to copy real life.
- Ⓒ They are boring.
- Ⓓ They are always about good things.

7 How does the speaker say that computer games are a problem?

- Ⓐ He compares young and older children.
- Ⓑ He compares old video games to new games.
- Ⓒ He lists the problems of modern games.
- Ⓓ He gives reasons why computer games are advanced.

8 Listen to part of the talk. Then answer the question.
Why does the speaker say this: 🎧

- Ⓐ To tell how computer games take away time
- Ⓑ To show how much fun computer games are to play
- Ⓒ To show how computer games teach us about real life
- Ⓓ To explain why some computer games are unpopular

Mini Test 2

9 What is the teacher talking about?

- Ⓐ Problem with cars
- Ⓑ Old tires on cars
- Ⓒ Making new tires
- Ⓓ Solving the old tire problem

10 How can we use old tires?

- Ⓐ By cutting them up and making new roads
- Ⓑ By storing them somewhere far away
- Ⓒ By putting them on new roads
- Ⓓ By burning them in the open

11 What comparison is made between old and new methods?

- Ⓐ No difference in method
- Ⓑ Uses of the old tires
- Ⓒ Changes in tire technology
- Ⓓ Colors of old tires

12 Why does the teacher mention special factories?

- Ⓐ To describe the tire making process
- Ⓑ To explain how to make better roads
- Ⓒ To show how to get rid of old tires safely
- Ⓓ To explain the environmental effects of tires

Mini Test 3

TOEFL Listening

TOEFL Listening

1. What is the conversation mainly about?
   - Ⓐ Popularity of music videos
   - Ⓑ Making of music videos
   - Ⓒ History of music videos
   - Ⓓ Who makes music videos

2. According to the conversation, what is true about music videos?
   - Ⓐ Music videos and MTV were a very good match.
   - Ⓑ The Beatles made a short film on music videos.
   - Ⓒ Music videos and MTV started at different times.
   - Ⓓ Mike Nesmith and MTV were not very popular.

3. What comparison is made between the Beatles' and Nesmith's video?
   - Ⓐ The popularity of the video
   - Ⓑ The cost of making the video
   - Ⓒ The length of the video
   - Ⓓ The number of people that watched the video

4. Listen again to part of the conversation. Then answer the question. What does the man mean when he says this: 🎧
   - Ⓐ People think music videos were too long.
   - Ⓑ People think music videos are exciting.
   - Ⓒ People think music videos are about movies.
   - Ⓓ People think music videos were around for a long time.

Mini Test 3 143

Mini Test 3

TOEFL Listening

5 What is the talk mainly about?

    Ⓐ The customs of native Americans
    Ⓑ How white Americans respected the natives
    Ⓒ The relationship between the native and white Americans
    Ⓓ How the Pilgrims survived winter

6 What is implied about the Indians?

    Ⓐ She thinks that they suffered.
    Ⓑ She thinks that they were bad.
    Ⓒ She thinks that they were not brave.
    Ⓓ She thinks that they won the war.

7 What did the Pilgrims learn from the Indians?

    Ⓐ They learned to use slaves.
    Ⓑ They learned to fight and kill.
    Ⓒ They learned to build homes.
    Ⓓ They learned how to keep warm and grow food.

8 How does the teacher discuss the two groups?

    Ⓐ By comparing the origins of the two groups
    Ⓑ By discussing how their friendship changed
    Ⓒ By explaining why the two groups fought
    Ⓓ By showing how the two groups helped each other

Mini Test 3

TOEFL Listening

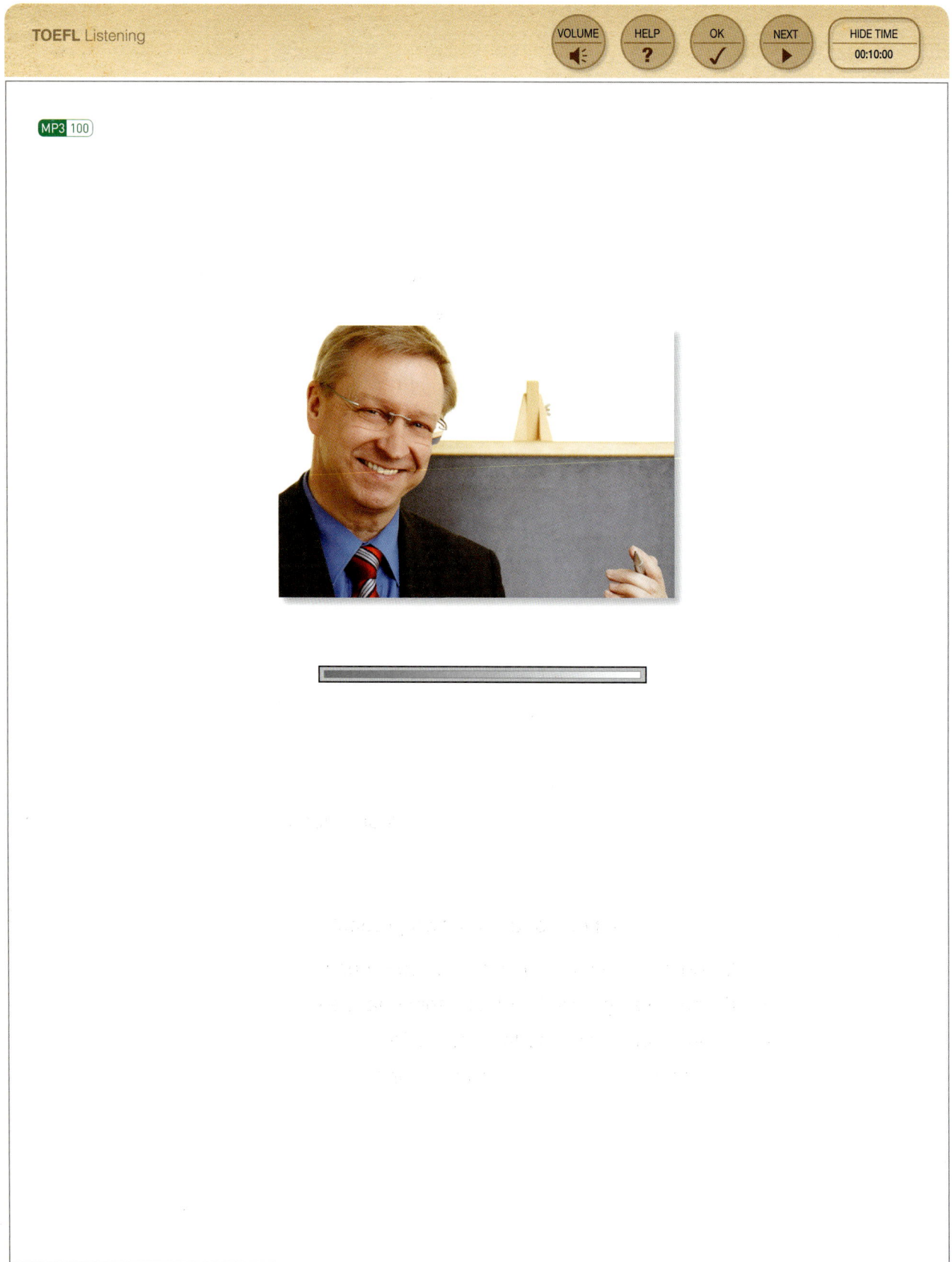

9 What is the talk mainly about?

Ⓐ The founding of Mongolia
Ⓑ Going to war
Ⓒ East Asia and Europe
Ⓓ Genghis Khan as a ruler

10 According to the talk, what is true about Genghis Khan?
Tick in the correct box.

	Yes	No
Ⓐ He lost many wars.		
Ⓑ He was a fair ruler.		
Ⓒ He forced people to change the way they live.		
Ⓓ He ruled from East Asia to Europe.		

11 Listen again to part of the talk. Then answer the question.
Why does the speaker say this:

Ⓐ To emphasize that Mongols were bad
Ⓑ To introduce another side of the Mongols
Ⓒ To show that Mongols were bad fighters
Ⓓ To state that Mongols did not like to fight

12 How does the speaker explain Genghis Khan?

Ⓐ By mentioning what he did as a ruler
Ⓑ By giving an example of stories from his childhood
Ⓒ By showing how cruel he was to other people
Ⓓ By comparing him to other rulers

Final iBT

http://www.finalibt.co.kr

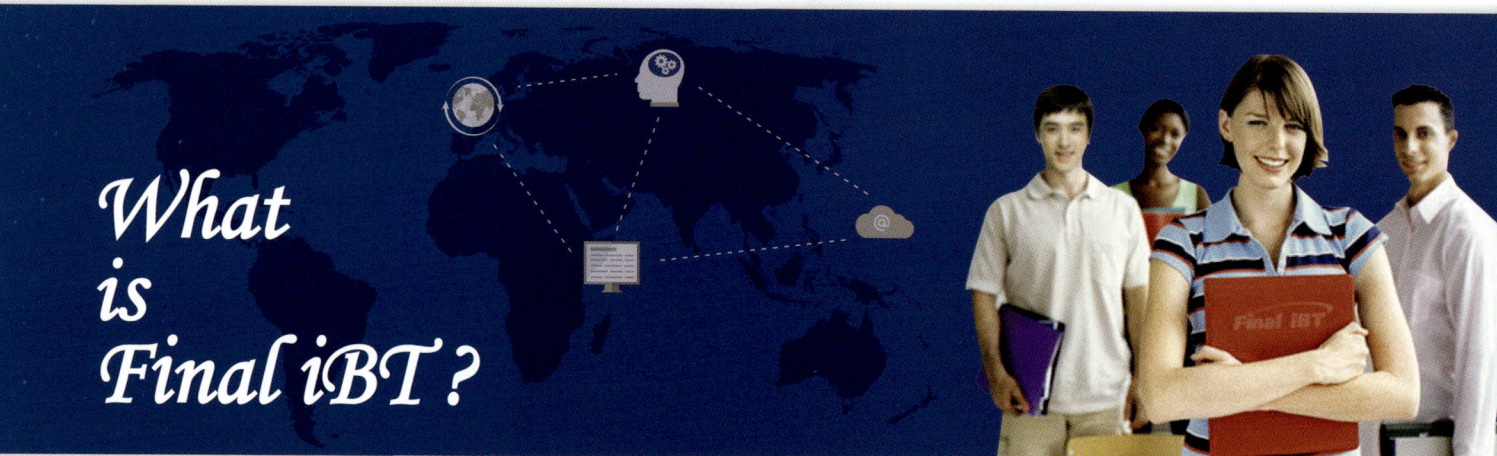

What is Final iBT?

Final iBT는 TOEFL 시험을 준비하는 학습자를 위한 완벽한 준비 도구로서 실제 IBT시험을 치르는 것과 같은 full-length의 연습테스트를 제공합니다. 지난 시험들을 통해 철저히 분석된 문제들을 연습하게 되며 48시간 이내에 점수를 받아볼 수 있습니다.

시험을 마친 후 상세한 그래프와 함께 자신의 점수를 분석할 수 있습니다. 또한 자신이 풀었던 문제와 답뿐만 아니라 Reading, Listening, Speaking, Writing의 스크립트를 제공받아 철저한 복습이 가능합니다.
Final iBT는 토플 모의 시험으로써 토플 준비를 위한 완벽한 학습 자료가 될 것입니다.

시험 구성

: 시험 구성은 다음과 같습니다.

Level	Test Version	Questions (문항)			
		Reading	Listening	Speaking	Writing
고급	Full	39~42	34	6	2
	Short	14~28	17	3	1
	Half (R/L)	39~42	34	X	X
	Half (S/W)	X	X	6	2
초급	Short	21~24	13	2	1

* 총 40회분의 시험이 제공됩니다.

http://www.finalibt.co.kr

PERFECT SOLUTION for **TOEFL Junior**

MP3파일 무료제공 http://www.linguaforum.com

LinguaForum

Chapter 1
Entertainment
/ Main Idea

Overview   p.10

Sample Question: (A)

Basic Drills 1   p.12

1. (A)   2. (B)   3. (B)

1. M: Hey, Lauren. Did you see the game last night?
   W: Of course. We won the game by 2 to 1.
   M: Yeah, it's not a bad score.
   W: I think the defense was weak.
   M: That's right, but we still get to go into the next World Cup.
   M: 로렌, 어젯밤에 경기 봤어?
   W: 물론이지. 우리가 2:1로 이겼잖아.
   M: 그래, 나쁜 점수는 아니지.
   W: 내 생각엔 수비가 약했던 것 같아.
   M: 맞아, 하지만 아직은 다음 월드컵에 갈 수 있잖아.

2. M: The show was wonderful! I feel so happy for the couple.
   M: Calm down, Jane. It's only a movie.
   W: I know it's a movie, but it was very romantic.
   M: I thought it had too much love. I prefer action movies.
   M: 영화 멋졌어! 그 연인들 너무 잘됐다.
   W: 진정해, 제인. 그냥 영화일 뿐이야.
   M: 영화인건 알아, 하지만 참 낭만적이야.
   W: 내 생각엔 그 영화에 사랑이 너무 넘쳐난 것 같아. 난 액션 영화가 더 좋아.

3. M: What do you want for dinner?
   W: I think I want to eat vegetables tonight.
   M: Are you on a diet? I wanted pizza.
   W: Well, eating just meat is not very healthy. Eating too much meat can lead to a heart attack. I don't want that.
   M: Alright. We'll eat what you want.
   M: 저녁 뭐 먹고 싶니?
   W: 오늘 밤에는 야채가 먹고 싶은데.
   M: 너 다이어트 하니? 난 피자가 먹고 싶은데.
   W: 글쎄, 고기만 먹는 건 건강에 별로 좋지 않아. 고기를 너무 많이 먹으면 심장마비에 걸릴 수도 있어. 난 그렇게 되고 싶지는 않아.
   M: 알았어. 네가 먹고 싶은 걸로 먹자.

Basic Drills 2   p.13

1. (A)   2. (B)   3. (B)

1. The internet can be used for many things. We can use it to send messages quickly. We can also play games on the internet.
   인터넷은 여러 가지 용도로 사용될 수 있다. 메시지를 재빨리 전하기 위해 사용할 수도 있고, 우리는 인터넷을 통해 게임을 할 수도 있다.

2. Inline skating is a fun sport. It can also be very dangerous if you do not wear your kneepads. Be safe when skating.
   인라인 스케이트는 재미있는 스포츠이다. 그렇지만 무릎 보호대를 착용하지 않으면 아주 위험할 수도 있다. 스케이트를 탈 때는 안전에 유의하자.

3. W: Did you watch the movie, "*Titanic*" on television last night?
   M: No, I didn't. Was it good?
   W: It was great. You missed a good movie.
   W: 어젯밤에 TV에서 '타이타닉' 봤니?
   M: 아니, 안 봤어. 재미있었니?
   W: 대단했어. 좋은 영화를 놓쳤네.

Listening Practice ① p.14

1. (D)   2. (A)

Many people watch comedy on television and comedians are getting more popular every day. However, it is hard work to be a comedian.

There are many types of comedians. The most common are called stand-up comedians. They only talk to make people laugh.

Comedians have to study other comedians and write new jokes. They practice for hours and make sure that they are funny to a broad audience. If they are not funny, people insult them. This is a comedian's worst nightmare.

The next time we see comedians, remember that it is a very hard job. Let's laugh a little louder for them.

많은 사람들이 텔레비전에서 코미디를 보는 것을 좋아하고 코미디언은 날마다 점점 더 인기가 높아진다. 그러나 코미디언이 되는 것은 어려운 일이다.

코미디언의 종류에는 여러 가지가 있다. 가장 일반적인 것은 '스탠드업 코미디언'이라고 불린다. 그들은 말로만 사람을 웃긴다.

코미디언은 다른 코미디언을 연구해서 새로운 농담을 써야 한다. 몇 시간 동안 연습해서 대중을 확실히 웃길 수 있도록 해야 한다. 만약 재미가 없다면 사람들은 그들을 욕한다. 이게 바로 코미디언에게는 최악의 상황인 것이다.

다음에 코미디언을 보게 된다면 그것이 힘든 직업이라는 것을 기억하자. 그리고 그들을 위해서 좀더 큰소리로 웃어보자.

Listening Practice ② p.15

1. (B)   2. (C)

W: Look at those clowns on the bicycle. They are going to fall!
M: Calm down. It's all part of the show.
W: Are you sure? They look like they are going to fall. They have a big bucket, and it looks like it's full of water.
M: I'm sure they have practiced many times. The bucket is probably empty. I am sure it is easy for them to ride like that.
W: But it looks so real. The clowns look like they are really carrying water. I don't want to get wet.
M: So you still think it is real? I guess the clowns have really practiced hard.

W: 저기 어릿광대가 자전거 타는 것 좀 봐. 저러다 넘어지겠다.
M: 진정해. 그것은 전부 공연의 일부일 뿐이야.
W: 확실해? 넘어질 것처럼 보이는데. 큰 양동이도 들고 있는데 그 안에 물이 가득 찬 것 같아.
M: 분명히 여러 번 연습 했을 거야. 아마 양동이 안에는 물도 없을 거고 분명 저렇게 타는 것도 저 사람들에겐 쉬운 일이야.
W: 하지만 너무 진짜 같다. 광대들이 진짜로 물을 나르고 있는 것처럼 보이는데. 난 젖기 싫어.
M: 그래서 아직도 저게 진짜라고 생각하는 거야? 저 광대들 진짜 열심히 연습했나 보다.

Listening Practice ③ p.16

1. (C)   2. (D)

There are many fun things in amusement parks. Roller coasters and rides are always popular. New roller coasters and rides get faster all the time. New technology pushes rides to higher speeds.

The fastest ride in Korea is the Gyrodrop. The Gyrodrop is very tall. It is a very fast ride. Many people sit on the Gyrodrop. It takes people up slowly. At the top, they enjoy the view for a few seconds. Then they race back down to the ground. Most people scream because it is so scary. The ride is only a few seconds, but it's very exciting!

놀이 공원에는 재미있는 것들이 많이 있다. 롤러코스터와 탑승기구들은 언제나 인기가 있다. 새로운 롤러코스터와 놀이기구들은 항상 점점 더 빨라진다. 신기술은 놀이기구의 속도를 높여준다.

한국에서 가장 빠른 놀이기구는 자이로드롭이라고 한다. 자이로드롭은 아주 높다. 그것은 아주 빠른 기구이다. 많은 사람들은 자이로드롭에 앉는다. 그 기구는 사람들을 천천히 올린다. 정상에서 그들은 몇 초 동안 경치를 즐긴다. 그리고 나서 다시 땅으로 질주한다. 대부분의 사람들은 무서워서 비명을 지른다. 탑승 시간은 몇 초 동안이지만 아주 신난다!

Listening Practice ④ p.17

1. (B) 2. (D)

Many children around the world know Disneyland. Mickey Mouse, Donald Duck, Cinderella and many other characters live there. Would you like to visit Disneyland? There are many things to do in Disneyland. You can get on fun rides and see your favorite Disney characters. You can shake hands and take pictures with them.

Disneyland is in Los Angeles, California. It is always sunny and bright in Los Angeles. You can have fun during the day. At night, you can watch the light parade. The light parade decorates everything with lights.

전 세계 많은 어린이들이 디즈니랜드를 알고 있다. 미키 마우스, 도날드 덕, 신데렐라 등 많은 다른 캐릭터들이 그곳에 살고 있다. 디즈니랜드에 가고 싶은가? 디즈니랜드에선 할 것들이 많다. 재미있는 기구들을 탈 수도 있고 좋아하는 디즈니 캐릭터들을 볼 수 있다. 그들과 악수하고 사진도 찍을 수 있다.

디즈니랜드는 캘리포니아 로스앤젤레스에 있다. 로스앤젤레스는 항상 맑고 화창하다. 낮 동안에는 신나게 놀 수 있다. 그리고 밤에는 불빛 퍼레이드를 구경할 수 있다. 불빛 퍼레이드는 모든 것을 불빛으로 장식한다.

iBT Practice 1 p.18

1. (A) 2. (C) 3. (A) 4. (D)

1-2.

Listen to the conversation between two friends.

W: Have you heard of Bruce Lee?
M: Oh, everybody knows him. He was an actor in the 1970s. He was the best kung-fu actor. He was fast, strong and an excellent fighter.
W: Yes, that is Bruce Lee. Koreans call him Lee So-Ryong.
M: Right, that's him. He lived in Hong Kong. He moved to the US when he was 18. He was a kung-fu teacher. Many of his students were actors. One of his students told a TV producer about Bruce.
W: So that's when he filmed the "Green Hornet." He was so fast.
M: That show was not very popular, but it made Bruce very famous. Later, he went to Hong Kong, but he only made a few movies. He died as a young man.

W: '브루스 리'라고 들어봤어?
M: 아, 그 사람은 누구나 알지. 그는 1970년대 배우였어. 최고의 쿵후 배우였지. 그는 빠르고 강하고 뛰어난 격투가였어.
W: 그래, 그 사람이 브루스 리야. 한국인들은 그를 이소룡이라고 불러.
M: 맞아. 그는 홍콩에서 태어나서 18살 때 미국으로 갔지. 그는 쿵후 사범이었어. 그의 제자들 중 많은 사람들이 배우였지. 그들 중 한 사람이 TV 제작자에게 브루스 리 얘기를 했어.
W: 그래서 그때 찍은 게 '그린 호넷'이지. 정말 빠르던데.
M: 그 영화는 별로 인기가 없었지만 브루스 리를 유명하게 만들었지. 나중에 홍콩에 갔지만 몇 편의 영화 밖에 찍지 못했어. 그는 젊은 나이에 죽었어.

3-4.

Listen to the conversation between two friends.

M: We are going to Seoul Land this weekend. We will bring our dog, Mimi, too. A friend of mine told me that there are many kinds of flowers.
W: Yes, the park is covered with flowers by now. If you go there, visit the zoo as well.
M: What kind of animals are in the zoo?
W: Tigers, lions, elephants, bears ... but don't worry. They are in their cages.
M: What about birds? I love birds.
W: Sure, you can also see many different birds.
M: Great! Do you know any nice restaurants in Seoul Land?
W: Yes, there is a delicious Korean restaurant in the park. They serve rice and vegetables which they have grown. Their meat and fish dishes are good too. Make sure you go there.

M: 우리 이번 주말에 서울랜드에 갈거야. 강아지 미미도 데리고 나올 거야. 친구 중 하나가 그러는데 거기엔 많은 종류의 꽃들이 있대.
W: 그래, 지금쯤 공원 전체가 꽃으로 뒤덮여 있어. 거기 가게 되면 동물원도 가봐.
M: 동물원에는 어떤 동물들이 있는데?
W: 호랑이, 사자, 코끼리, 곰… 하지만, 걱정하지 마. 그 동물들

은 우리 안에 갇혀 있어.
M: 새들도 있니? 난 새가 참 좋은데.
W: 물론 다른 종류의 새들도 많이 볼 수 있어.
M: 잘됐다! 서울랜드 안에 근사한 식당 아니?
W: 그럼, 공원 안에 맛있는 한식집이 있는데 그 집은 쌀밥과 직접 기른 야채를 제공해. 육류와 생선 요리도 맛있어. 꼭 가도록 해.

iBT Practice 2   p.20

1. (D)   2. (B)   3. (A)   4. (A)

1-2.

Listen to the speaker.

Rap was the most important new music in the 1990s. Black music has always been important in the area of pop music. Rap is different from other music. It is because rap singers talk more than they sing. They speak their words fast over music. Their words are like poems. They always rhyme with the next line. This is why rap singers are sometimes called poets.

Musicians take sounds from different records and create music for their lyrics. Rap was the music of the city streets. The words were about hard life in the city. Rap changed pop music in the 1990s.

랩은 1990년대에 가장 중요한 새로운 음악이었다. 흑인음악은 대중음악 분야에서 항상 중요한 장르였다. 랩은 다른 음악과는 다르다. 왜냐하면 랩 가수는 노래보다는 말을 더 많이 하기 때문이다. 그들은 음악에 맞춰 가사를 재빨리 말한다. 그 가사는 시와 같다. 그들은 가사의 운율을 맞춘다. 그래서 랩 가수를 때때로 시인이라고 부르기도 한다.

뮤지션들은 다른 음반에서 소리를 뽑아내서 그들의 가사에 맞춰 음악을 창조한다. 랩은 거리의 음악이었다. 그 가사는 도시의 힘겨운 삶에 관한 것 이었다. 랩은 1990년대 대중음악을 변화시켰다.

3-4.

Listen to the conversation between two students.

W: Can you believe that guy? He wasn't funny at all.
M: Really? I couldn't stop laughing! His jokes were very funny.
W: I don't think it's funny. He should not talk about his own mother that way.
M: That's what stand-up comedians do. They make fun of others and copy other people.
W: Well, saying bad things about your own mother is bad. Telling other people about it is worse.
M: Don't be too upset. Everybody knows it was just a joke. I'm sure his mother understands.
W: I know, but my mom wouldn't be happy if I did that.
M: That is because you are not a comedian. If you were a comedian, I am sure your mom would understand, too.

W: 저 남자 왜 저러는 거지? 전혀 재미있지 않던데.
M: 정말? 난 웃음이 멈추질 않던데! 그 농담은 너무 재미있었어.
W: 나는 재미있는지 모르겠더라. 자기 엄마를 그런 식으로 얘기하면 안되지.
M: 스탠드업 코미디언이 그렇지 뭐. 다른 사람들을 놀리고 흉내 내는 건데.
W: 글쎄, 자기 엄마에 대해 험담을 하는 건 나쁜 일이지. 그 얘길 다른 사람들에게 하는 건 더 나쁘고.
M: 너무 기분 상하지 마. 다들 그게 농담인 줄 알고 있어. 그 사람 어머니도 이해하실 꺼야.
W: 알아, 하지만 내가 저렇게 했다면 우리 어머니는 기분 나쁘셨을걸.
M: 그건 네가 코미디언이 아니기 때문이지. 네가 만약 코미디언이라면 분명히 너희 어머니도 이해하실 꺼야.

Word Review   p.26

1. empty	2. scream
3. decorate	4. cage
5. ride	6. perform
7. release	8. poet
9. make sure	10. made fun of
11. calm down	12. shook hands

Chapter 2
Jobs
/ Supporting Detail

Overview   p.30

Sample Question: (B)

Basic Drills 1   p.32

1. (C)   2. (B)   3. (B)

1. W: I got a part-time job in the supermarket.
   M: That's great. When are you going to start working?
   W: Day after tomorrow. I'm really excited. This is my first job.
   M: I'm happy to hear that. Maybe I should look for a job, too.

   W: 나 슈퍼마켓에서 시간제로 일하게 됐어.
   M: 대단하다. 일은 언제부터 시작하는데?
   W: 내일 모레부터. 정말 떨려. 내 첫 번째 일이거든.
   M: 그거 잘 됐다. 아마 나도 일을 구해봐야 할것 같아.

2. M: I'm so tired. I had to move 20 boxes of fruits today.
   W: Wow! That's a lot. What kind of fruits were in the box? Apples? Oranges?
   M: There were a lot of apples in the boxes.
   W: You must have been really busy.

   M: 정말 피곤해. 오늘 과일 20상자를 옮겨야 했어
   W: 와! 많이 옮겼다. 상자 안에 무슨 과일이 있었는데? 사과? 오렌지?
   M: 상자 안에는 많은 사과가 있었어.
   W: 너 정말 바빴겠구나.

3. W: I think it must be exciting for Sally to be a photographer.
   M: I think so too. She travels with her camera and takes pictures of wild animals.
   W: Maybe we should become photographers too.
   M: Yes, I don't like sitting in a chair all day long.

   W: 샐리가 사진작가가 되면 정말 신날 것 같아.
   M: 나도 그렇게 생각해. 카메라를 들고 여행을 다니면서 야생동물 사진도 찍고.
   W: 우리도 사진작가가 돼야겠다!
   M: 그래, 하루 종일 의자에 앉아 있는 건 싫어.

Basic Drills 2   p.33

1. (A)   2. (B)   3. (A)

1. There are many ways a young person can get pocket money. It can be at home or outside. We can look for work at home. We can cut the grass or wash the car. We can also look for work outside. Neighbors might need someone to help them.

   젊은 사람이 용돈을 버는 방법은 여러 가지가 있다. 집 안 또는 집 밖에서도 벌 수 있다. 집안에서 일거리를 찾을 수 있다. 우리는 잔디를 깎거나 세차를 할 수 있다. 밖에서 일을 구할 수 도 있다. 이웃 사람들 중에는 자기들을 도와 줄 사람을 필요로 할지도 모른다.

2. Some people like to have safe and quiet jobs. Jobs in the office are usually quiet and safe. Other people like exciting jobs. Outdoor jobs are usually exciting and sometimes dangerous. We must always do our best in anything we do.

   어떤 사람들은 안전하고 조용한 일을 하고 싶어한다. 사무실에서 하는 일은 주로 조용하고 안전하다. 다른 사람들은 흥미진진한 일을 하고 싶어한다. 밖에서 하는 일은 주로 흥미진진하지만 때로는 위험하다. 우리는 우리가 하는 어떤 일이든 최선을 다해야 한다.

3. W: It must be so much fun to be a professional dancer.
   M: Yes, but you need a lot of energy. You also need a lot of practice because you might perform in public.

W: That is true, but I still think it would be so much fun.
W: 직업 무용가가 되면 정말 재미있을 거야.
M: 그래, 하지만 많은 열정이 필요해. 대중들 앞에서 공연을 할 수도 있을 테니 많은 연습이 필요할 테고.
W: 사실이야, 그래도 내 생각엔 아주 재미있을 것 같아.

Listening Practice ❶ p.34

1. (A)   2. (B)

W: Have you heard of Harley-Davidson?
M: Of course! They are the most famous motorcycle company in the world. Even people who do not like motorcycles know Harley-Davidson.
W: That's right. The founders were William Harley and Arthur Davidson. Like most companies, they started off really small.
M: So, how did a small company get so famous?
W: They won a motorcycle race in 1905.
M: Wow! I didn't know that. What I know is that their motorcycles are so special that even the sound is copyrighted.
W: Yes, that makes them a very special motorcycle company. I love everything about Harley-Davidson. I would love to ride one.
W: '할리 데이비슨'이라고 들어봤니?
M: 물론이지! 세계에서 제일 유명한 모터사이클 회사잖아. 모터사이클을 좋아하지 않는 사람들도 할리 데이비슨은 안다고.
W: 맞아. 설립자는 윌리엄 할리와 아더 데이비슨이었지. 다른 회사들처럼 처음에는 작은 회사에서 출발했어.
M: 그럼 그렇게 작은 회사가 어떻게 그렇게 유명해졌지?
W: 1905년 모터사이클 경주에서 우승을 했어.
M: 와! 그건 몰랐네. 내가 알고 있는 것은 그 모터사이클은 아주 독특해서 소리에 저작권이 있다는 것이야.
W: 그래, 그것 때문에 아주 특별한 모터사이클 회사가 되었지. 할리데이비슨이라면 다 좋아. 나도 하나 타보고 싶어.

Listening Practice ❷ p.35

1. (C)   2. (B)

W: Who do you think is the best stuntman?
M: I say it's Evel Knievel. He was the most popular stuntman in the US.
W: Yes, I heard of him. He was that guy on the motorcycle, right? Why is he different from others?
M: It was probably because he did the longest jumps. He also hurt himself a lot. He fell off his motorcycle after he landed when setting the record of a 41-meter jump.
W: How badly did he hurt himself?
M: Well, he broke a total of 35 bones in his life as a stuntman.
W: Yes, I remember hearing that he once had to stay three months in hospital. He still did jumps after that.
W: 네 생각엔 누가 최고의 스턴트맨인 것 같니?
M: Evel Knievel 인 것 같아. 그는 미국에서 가장 인기 있는 스턴트맨이야.
W: 맞아, 나도 그 사람에 대해 들어봤어. 모터사이클 타던 사람 맞지? 왜 그 사람은 다른 사람들과 다르다는 거지?
M: 아마 그 이유는 그가 가장 긴 점프를 했기 때문일 거야. 또 많이 다치기도 했지. 41미터 점프 기록을 세우고 착지를 하면서 모터사이클에서 떨어졌어.
W: 얼마나 많이 다쳤는데?
M: 글쎄, 스턴트맨으로 살면서 총 35개의 뼈가 부러졌어.
W: 맞아, 한번은 석 달 동안 병원에 입원해야 했었다는 얘기도 들은 것 같아. 그래도 그 이후에 계속 점프를 했대.

Listening Practice ❸ p.36

1. (A)   2. (C)

  Sumo is a very popular sport in Japan. In Japan, sumo wrestlers are very famous. They make lots of money. Sumo wrestlers are very big. Some sumo wrestlers weigh over 180 kilograms! They have to eat a lot. They also have to practice for many years to become a sumo wrestler.

Every sumo wrestler wants to be the Grand Champion. The Grand Champion is the most popular wrestler in Japan. When he comes out in public, many people treat him like a superstar. All the sumo wrestlers in the world meet every year to try and become the Grand Champion.

일본에서 스모는 매우 인기 있는 스포츠이다. 스모선수들은 일본에서 아주 유명하다. 그들은 많은 돈을 번다. 스모선수들은 아주 크다. 어떤 스모선수들은 180킬로그램이 넘는다. 그들은 많이 먹어야 한다. 또한 스모선수들은 선수가 되기 위해 수년간 훈련을 해야 한다.

모든 스모선수들은 그랜드 챔피언(천하 장사)이 되고 싶어 한다. 그랜드 챔피언은 일본에서 가장 인기 있는 선수이다. 그가 대중들 앞에 나오면 사람들은 그를 슈퍼 스타처럼 대한다. 전 세계 모든 스모선수들은 매년 그랜드 챔피언에 도전하기 위해 모인다.

Listening Practice 4 p.37

> 1. (B)   2. (D)

M: We don't need lawyers. Lawyers only think about money.
W: That is not true. Lawyers help poor people too. They work for free.
M: People still call them "sharks" because they always hunt for money.
W: Lawyers do not always look for money. They are very helpful. Lawyers can help people fight bad people using law. Lawyers can also protect people if they need it.
M: But bad people can also have lawyers. It takes a long time for lawyers to fight.
W: They fight because they need to fight with law. Law can be very tricky. Lawyers help us understand the law better.
M: Well, let's agree that there are good and bad lawyers, then.

M: 변호사는 필요 없어. 변호사는 돈 생각만 하잖아.
W: 그렇지 않아. 변호사들은 가난한 사람들을 도와 주기도 해. 무료로도 일을 하지.
M: 사람들은 여전히 그들을 '상어'라고 불러. 왜냐하면 그들은 언제나 돈을 쫓아 다니기 때문이지.
W: 변호사들이 항상 돈만 밝히는 건 아니야. 그들은 아주 도움을 많이 주지. 변호사는 법을 이용해서 사람들이 나쁜 사람들과 싸우도록 도울 수 있어. 변호사는 사람들이 필요하다면 그들을 보호할 수도 있어.
M: 하지만 나쁜 사람들도 변호사를 내세울 수가 있어. 변호사가 싸우는 데 오랜 시간이 걸려.
W: 그들은 법과 싸우기 위해서 싸우는 거야. 법이란 매우 까다로울 수 있어. 변호사들은 우리가 법을 더 잘 이해할 수 있도록 도와줘.
M: 글쎄, 그럼 그냥 좋은 변호사도 있고 나쁜 변호사도 있다는 걸로 하자.

iBT Practice 1 p.38

> 1. (B)   2. Yes: (A), (C) / No: (B), (D)
> 3. (A)   4. (C)

1-2.

Listen to a conversation between two people.

W: Is it good to be a doctor?
M: It is both good and bad. Being a doctor, I have many responsibilities, but I must say that I am happy to be a doctor.
M: When are you happy being a doctor? Doctors seem to be busy all the time.
M: You are right. We are always busy. When people need help, they come to us. We help them get better quickly. Helping people can feel good.
W: Is that all? I thought it was good because of money.
M: I don't think so. We become doctors because we want to help others.
W: What else makes you happy being a doctor?
M: When we tell family and friends some good news about a patient, it is a great feeling.

W: 의사가 된다는 건 좋은가요?
M: 좋은 점도 있고 나쁜 점도 있지요. 의사로서 많은 책임이 생기지만, 의사가 돼서 행복하다고 말해야겠군요.
W: 어떨 때 의사가 된 것이 기쁜가요? 의사들은 항상 바빠 보이던데.
M: 맞아요. 우린 항상 바빠요. 사람들은 도움이 필요할 때 우리에게 와요. 우리는 그들이 빨리 나을 수 있게 도와주죠. 사람

들을 돕는 게 기뻐요.
W: 그게 다예요? 내 생각엔 돈 때문에 기뻤을 것 같은데.
M: 전 그렇게 생각 안 해요. 우리는 다른 사람들을 돕고 싶어서 의사가 된 거예요.
W: 의사가 돼서 뭐가 또 기쁘죠?
M: 환자의 가족과 친구들에게 환자에 대한 기쁜 소식을 전할 때, 그때 기분이 좋죠.

3-4.

Listen to the teacher in the classroom.

There are many nurses in a hospital. They seem to be everywhere. Did you know that there are nurses even in the operating room? For example, doctors need very clean hands for the operation. This is why nurses must prepare many things.

During the operation, doctors concentrate on their work. Nurses must concentrate on the machines that show everything about the patient. Nurses play an important role in the operating room.

After the operation, nurses stay with the patient. They make sure that the patient is doing OK. Nurses check on the patient often until the patient leaves the hospital. Let's not forget to thank the nurses next time.

병원에는 많은 간호사들이 있다. 그들은 사방에 있는 것처럼 보인다. 수술실에도 간호사들이 있다는 걸 알고 있는가? 예를 들면, 의사들은 수술을 위해 손이 깨끗해야 할 필요가 있다. 그렇기 때문에 간호사들이 여러 가지 준비를 하는 것이다.

수술 중에 의사는 자기 일에만 집중해야 한다. 간호사들은 환자에 대한 모든 상태를 보여주는 기계들에 집중을 해야만 한다. 간호사들은 수술실에서 중요한 역할을 담당한다.

수술 후에 간호사는 환자 옆에 있다. 환자의 상태가 좋은지 확인을 한다. 간호사들은 환자가 병원을 떠날 때까지 자주 환자들의 상태를 점검한다. 다음부터 간호사들에게 감사하는 것을 잊지 말자.

iBT Practice 2 p.40

| 1. (B) | 2. (D) | 3. (C) | 4. (B) |

1-2.

Listen to the teacher in the classroom.

Many people ride in airplanes. But not many people know how to fly a big plane. Pilots know how to control the airplane. They train very hard to become a pilot. Pilots are responsible for everyone in the plane.

Before each flight, pilots check the inside and outside of the plane. They must make sure that there is nothing wrong with the plane.

Pilots train for many different problems. This is why everyone listens to them in an emergency. Pilots are the most important people in the airplane. They must not get sick when flying the plane, so they eat food that is specially prepared for them.

Do you want to become a pilot one day?

많은 사람들은 비행기를 탄다. 하지만 그 큰 비행기가 어떻게 나는지 아는 사람은 많지 않다. 비행사는 비행기를 조종하는 방법을 알고 있다. 그들은 비행사가 되기 위해 힘든 훈련을 한다. 비행사는 비행기 안에 있는 모든 사람들을 책임진다.

매번 비행 전에 비행사는 비행기의 내부와 외부를 점검한다. 비행기에 아무런 문제가 없는지 확인을 해야 한다.

비행사는 여러 가지 비상사태에 대비해 훈련을 받는다. 그래서 많은 사람들은 비상사태 시에는 그들의 말을 따르게 된다. 비행사는 비행기에서 가장 중요한 사람이다. 그들은 비행기를 조종할 때 아파서는 안 된다. 그래서 그들은 그들만을 위해 특별히 마련된 음식을 먹는다.

당신도 언젠가 비행사가 되고 싶은가?

3-4.

Listen to the student in a classroom.

My aunt has a small shop next to a bus stop. She sells many things in such a small space – drinks, newspapers, food, and snacks – almost everything! People are always buying something, so she is always busy.

In the morning, a lot of people buy newspapers. Some people need to recharge their bus pass. Some people buy sandwiches to eat. When school is over in the afternoon, a lot of students buy ice cream and snacks. They buy food on the way back home, or on the way to an institute. In the evening, a lot of people from the office come to buy drinks and chewing gum.

My aunt can only rest when she comes back

home. It must be so tiring to sell things every day for so long! But my aunt says that she enjoys working in the shop.

우리 이모는 버스 정류장 옆 작은 가게를 갖고 계신다. 그녀는 아주 작은 공간에서 여러 가지 - 음료수, 신문, 음식, 간식 - 거의 모든 것을 판다. 사람들은 항상 무언가를 사고 있고 그래서 그녀는 항상 바쁘다.

아침에는 많은 사람들이 신문을 산다. 어떤 사람들은 버스 카드를 충전한다. 어떤 사람들은 샌드위치를 사먹는다. 오후에 학교가 끝나면 많은 학생들이 아이스크림과 과자를 산다. 그들은 집에 돌아가는 길이나 학원에 가는 길에 먹을 것을 산다. 저녁에는 회사에서 많은 사람들이 음료수나 껌을 사러 온다.

우리 이모는 집에 돌아와서야 쉴 수 있다. 매일 그렇게 오랫동안 물건을 파는 일은 정말 피곤할 것이다. 하지만 우리 숙모님은 가게에서 일하는 것이 언제나 즐겁다고 하신다.

Word Review   p.46

1. protect	2. emergency
3. lawyer	4. neighbor
5. land	6. professional
7. prepare	8. responsibility
9. on the way	10. for free
11. in public	12. look for

Chapter 3
Do's and Don'ts
/ Organization

Overview   p.50

Sample Question: (A)

Basic Drills 1   p.52

1. (B)-(C)-(A)   2. (C)-(B)-(A)   3. (A)

1. Last summer, we went to a three-day camp. We made many new friends and learned a lot of things. We learned to ride horses on the first day. We painted pictures the next day. Many kids swam in the lake on the last day. We had a very good time.

   우리는 지난 여름 3일간 캠프를 갔었다. 우린 많은 친구들을 사귀었고 많은 것들을 배웠다. 첫째 날 우리는 말 타는 법을 배웠다. 다음 날에는 그림을 그렸다. 마지막 날에 많은 아이들이 호수에서 수영을 했다. 정말 즐거운 시간이었다.

2. Driving a car can be a lot of fun. But there are some things we have to do before we can drive a car on the road. First, we need to pass a written test. Then, we must practice driving on the road with a driving instructor. Finally, we need to pass a driving test.

   자동차 운전은 재미 있을 것 같다. 하지만 도로 위에서 운전을 할 수 있기 전에 몇 가지 해야 할 것들이 있다. 먼저 필기 시험을 통과해야 한다. 그리고 나서 우리는 운전 강사와 도로 주행 연습을 해야 한다. 마지막으로 주행 시험을 통과하면 된다.

3. Oranges taste sweet, but lemons taste very sour. This is because lemons have much more citric acid than oranges do. Oranges also have citric acid, but not as much as lemons. There

are also other fruits that have citric acid. Citric acid is very powerful. It is often used in kitchen soap to wash off oil and smell good.

오렌지는 달콤하다 하지만 레몬은 무척 시다. 그 이유는 레몬에는 오렌지 보다 구연산이 많기 때문이다. 오렌지에도 구연산은 있지만 레몬만큼 많지 않다. 다른 과일들에도 구연산은 있다. 구연산은 아주 강력하다. 그래서 구연산은 기름기를 제거하고 향을 좋게 하는 주방 세제를 만드는데 종종 이용된다.

Basic Drills 2   p.53

> 1. (B)   2. (A)   3. (B)

1. Doctors say that it is important to eat three full meals every day. Breakfast is the most important meal of the day. It is even more important to have a good breakfast than lunch or dinner. We should eat breakfast with a lot of fiber to help digestion throughout the day.

의사들은 매일 하루 세 끼를 다 먹는 것이 중요하다고 한다. 아침은 하루 중 가장 중요한 식사이다. 점심과 저녁보다 잘 차려진 아침을 먹는 것이 훨씬 더 중요하다. 하루 동안 소화를 도울 섬유질이 풍부한 아침식사를 먹어야 한다.

2. When you go camping, you should always remember a few important things. First, clean up your camp. Rubbish can be bad for the land. You should not start any fires. Many forest fires start this way. Don't keep food in your tent. Animals have an excellent sense of smell. They will smell the food and look for it in the tent.

야영을 할 때는 몇 가지 중요한 것들을 항상 기억해야 한다. 먼저 야영장을 청결히 해야 한다. 쓰레기는 토양에 해롭다. 어떠한 불도 피워서는 안 된다. 많은 산불이 이런 식으로 시작된다. 텐트 안에 음식을 두어서는 안 된다. 동물들은 후각이 뛰어나다. 그래서 음식 냄새를 맡고 텐트 안으로 음식을 찾으러 들어올지 모른다.

3. You should remember a few rules when going up a mountain. First, you should never go alone. If you are alone and fall, no one will know you are in trouble. You should also check your ropes before each climb. Your ropes must not break when you are using them. Finally, you should check the weather. You do not want to be on the mountain during a storm.

산에 올라갈 때는 몇 가지 규칙을 명심해야 한다. 먼저 절대로 혼자서 올라가서는 안 된다. 만약 혼자 있을 때 추락하면 아무도 당신이 곤경에 처했는지 알 수 없다. 또 매번 산을 오를 때 마다 밧줄을 점검해야 한다. 사용하는 동안 밧줄이 끊어지면 안 된다. 마지막으로 날씨를 확인하라. 폭풍우 속에서 산에 있고 싶진 않을 테니까.

Listening Practice ❶   p.54

> 1. (B)   2. (A)

Many of us enjoy eating. We must also remember our manners at the table. Table manners are important in any culture, and here are some.
First, when food enters our mouth, we should not make noise. We must be careful when eating noodles or soup. We should only eat small amounts at a time.

Second, we should always chew with our mouth closed. Lastly, once food has entered our mouth, we should not open or make any sound until the food is swallowed.

Western cultures have conversations during meals. But we must remember to chew and swallow the food in our mouth before we speak. If we have to speak when we still have food in our mouth, we should always cover our mouth to talk.

많은 사람들이 먹는 것을 좋아한다. 다른 사람들과 식사를 할 때 우리는 식사 예절을 명심해야 한다. 식사예절은 어느 문화에서든 중요하다. 그래서 몇 가지를 말해보겠다.

우선 입 안으로 음식이 들어오면 우리는 가능한 한 소리를 내지 말아야 한다. 국수나 스프를 먹을 때는 더 주의해야 한다. 한번에 적은 양만 먹는 것이 좋다.

두 번째는 항상 입을 다물고 음식을 씹어야 한다. 마지막으로 일단 음식이 입 안으로 들어오면 음식을 삼킬 때까지 입을 벌리거나 소리를 내서는 안 된다.

서양 문화에서는 식사 중 대화하는 것을 즐긴다. 하지만 말을 시작하기 전에 음식을 씹어서 삼키는 것을 명심하자. 아직 입 안에 음식이 있는데 말을 해야 한다면 말을 할 때 입을 가려야 한다.

Listening Practice ❷   p.55

1. (B)   2. (A)

Are the streets near your house dirty? The problem is probably littering. People throw their trash on the street. Littering is a big problem in many places.

One way to stop littering is to catch them and make them pay money. Paying money usually works well, but we need a lot of police to catch them.

Another way to stop littering is to put more trash cans on the streets. Most people are not bad people. They are just lazy. They don't want to carry their trash.

당신 집 주변 거리가 지저분한가? 아마도 문제는 사람들이 쓰레기를 버리기 때문일 것이다. 사람들은 자기 쓰레기를 거리에 버린다. 쓰레기 투기는 많은 곳에서 큰 문제가 된다.

쓰레기 투기를 막을 수 있는 한가지 방법으로 잡아서 벌금을 내게 하는 것이 있다. 벌금을 내게 하는 것은 대개는 효과가 좋지만 사람들을 적발하려면 많은 경찰이 필요하다.

쓰레기 투기를 막을 수 있는 다른 방법으로 거리에 쓰레기통을 더 만드는 것이 있다. 대부분의 사람들은 나쁜 사람들이 아니다. 그들은 그저 게으른 것뿐이다. 그들은 쓰레기를 들고 다니고 싶지 않은 것이다.

Listening Practice ❸   p.56

1. (C)   2. (D)

You probably know at least one bully in your school. They are very mean to other children. Bullies are usually big kids. They tease, hit and steal from other children. How would you stop a bully?

You can stay with your friends. Bullies are usually mean to only one person. They don't bully if you are with other people or if you are in places where teachers can see you.

You can always tell a teacher if a bully is disturbing you. Many kids don't tell teachers, but you should talk to them. A teacher can punish bullies or call their parents.

적어도 교내에 한 명의 싸움꾼은 알고 있을 것이다. 그들은 다른 아이들에게 못되게 군다. 싸움꾼은 주로 덩치가 큰 아이들이다. 그들은 다른 아이들을 놀리거나 때리고 물건을 훔친다. 그들을 막으려면 어떻게 해야 할까?

친구들과 함께 있어라. 싸움꾼은 주로 한 아이만 괴롭힌다. 당신이 다른 사람들과 함께 있거나, 선생님이 볼 수 있는 곳에 있으면 괴롭히지 않는다.

싸움꾼이 괴롭히면 선생님께 말하라. 많은 아이들이 선생님께 말을 하지 않지만, 말을 해야 한다. 선생님은 싸움꾼들을 벌 주거나 부모님을 부를 수 있다.

Listening Practice ❹   p.57

1. (D)   2. (A)

Cell phones are very convenient. Most people cannot think about life without cell phones. But we must also realize that there are manners when using cell phones.

We should be quiet when using the cell phone in public places. It is very rude to talk so loudly that other people can hear you. We should either tell the person to call back later, or talk quietly and not disturb other people.

We should always remember to switch off the phone in movies or shows. Nobody likes noisy people when they are enjoying something else. In foreign countries, people have to pay money if they get caught using the phone in shows.

휴대폰은 아주 편리하다. 대부분의 사람들이 휴대폰 없는 생활은 생각할 수 없을 것이다. 하지만 휴대폰을 사용할 때 지켜야 할 예의가 있다는 것도 명심해야 한다.

공공장소에서 휴대폰을 사용할 때는 조용히 해야 한다. 다른 사람들이 들릴 정도로 큰 소리로 이야기하는 것은 아주 무례한 일이다. 나중에 전화를 주겠다고 말을 하거나 조용히 통화를 해서 다른 사람들을 방해하지 않아야 한다.

영화나 공연 중에는 항상 휴대폰의 전원을 꺼야 한다. 다른 무엇인가를 즐기고 있을 때 어느 누구도 소란을 피우는 사람을 좋아하지 않는다. 외국에서는 공연 중에 통화를 하면 벌금을 물어야 한다.

iBT Practice 1

p.58

| 1. (B) | 2. (C) | 3. (C) | 4. (A) |

1-2.

Listen to the teacher in the classroom.

Do you exercise often? Sometimes we do not feel like exercising, but we must not be lazy and exercise often. There are many reasons to exercise.

Exercising keeps our body fit. When we exercise, many muscles in our body move and stay strong. Inner muscles, such as the heart and lungs, also need exercise. It is very important to exercise the heart to stay healthy when we get older.

Exercising will also make our minds fresh. Scientists proved that exercising and a healthy mind are related. People who exercise regularly will not feel tired easily when studying and sitting down for a long time. They will feel good about themselves.

당신은 운동을 자주 하는가? 간혹 운동을 하기가 싫어지지만 게을러지지 말고 자주 운동을 해야 한다. 운동을 해야 하는데는 많은 이유가 있다.

운동을 하면 몸이 건강하게 유지가 된다. 운동을 하면 우리 몸의 근육들이 많이 움직여 강해진다. 심장이나 폐 같은 내부 근육도 운동이 필요하다. 나이가 먹으면 심장을 건강히 유지하기 위해 운동을 하는 것이 매우 중요하다.

운동을 하면 우리의 마음도 상쾌해진다. 과학자들은 운동과 건강한 정신이 연관되어 있다는 것을 증명했다. 규칙적으로 운동하는 사람들은 오래 공부를 하거나 앉아 있어도 쉽게 피로해지지 않는다. 그들은 스스로에게 좋은 기분을 느끼게 된다.

3-4.

Listen to the speaker.

Many of us walk on the streets. When we walk outside, we must be careful and follow the rules.

We must always walk on the walkway. It is dangerous for people to walk on the road where the cars are speeding by. There are many others who walk on the walkway, so we should not suddenly stop or run.

We should always cross the road on the crosswalk. Even if the light is green, we should still look left and right to check for cars. Once we are on the crossing, we should walk quickly to the other side.

많은 사람들이 길을 걸어 다닌다. 밖에서 걸어 다닐 때 우리는 신중해야 하고 규칙을 지켜야 한다.

우리는 보도를 따라서 통행해야 한다. 차들이 질주하는 길로 다니는 것은 위험하다. 보행로 위에는 다른 사람들도 많이 있다. 따라서 우리는 갑자기 멈추거나 뛰어다녀서는 안 된다.

항상 횡단보도에서만 길을 건너야 한다. 초록색 불이 켜졌더라도 좌우를 살피고 차가 멈췄는지 확인을 해야 한다. 일단 길을 건너기 시작했으면 반대편으로 재빨리 건너야 한다.

iBT Practice 2

p.60

| 1. (B) | 2. (D) | 3. (A) | 4. (C) |

1-2.

Listen to the speaker.

Going to college is an important event. Preparing for college is not easy. You have to study a lot and take many tests. Today, children prepare early for college. They have to get good grades. Why is going to college important?

You need to go to college to learn about the world. You also meet many people and learn to socialize better. College prepares you for life ahead.

Some people want to go to college to get a job that they want to do. If you don't go to college, getting a job will be difficult. For example, do you want to become a doctor, a teacher or a nurse? Then you need to study very hard.

대학 진학은 중요한 일이다. 대학준비를 하는 것은 쉽지 않다. 많이 공부해야 하고 시험도 많이 봐야 한다. 요즘에는 아이들이 일찍부터 대학 준비를 한다. 그들은 좋은 점수를 따야 한다. 그렇다면 왜 대학 진학이 중요한 것일까?

세상에 대해 좀 더 배우기 위해선 대학에 갈 필요가 있다. 또 많은 사람들을 만나서 사회에 잘 적응하는 법을 배운다. 대학은 다가올 삶에 대한 준비를 시켜준다.

어떤 사람은 자기가 하고 싶은 직업을 얻기 위해서 대학에 진학 한다. 대학에 가지 않으면 직업을 얻기가 어려울 것이다. 예를 들어서, 의사, 선생님, 혹은 간호사가 되고 싶은가? 그렇다면 열심히 공부해야 한다.

3-4.
Listen to the conversation between two friends.

M: I hate separating rubbish like this. It's hard work.
W: It's not an easy task, but it is important for everyone. We are helping the world waste less and save energy.
M: Think about the energy to recycle. I think the energy used to make a new product or for recycling would be the same.
W: No, that is not true. Recycling factories use much less energy. They also do not use new materials to make new products.
M: Alright, I understand that now, but I want to know why we separate it.
W: Because there are different recycling factories for different materials. It saves a lot of time for everyone if we separate it now.

M: 이렇게 쓰레기 분리하는 거 싫어. 힘든 작업이야.
W: 쉬운 일이 아니지만 모두를 위해 중요한 일이야. 전 세계가 낭비를 줄이고 에너지를 절약할 수 있도록 하거든.
M: 재활용에 필요한 에너지를 생각해봐. 새로운 상품을 만들거나 재활용을 하는데 드는 에너지가 비슷할 것 같은데.
W: 아니야 그렇지 않아. 재활용 공장은 훨씬 더 적은 에너지를 사용해. 그리고 새로운 상품을 만드는데 새 재료를 쓰지 않아.
M: 알겠어, 이제 이해가 가지만 왜 우리가 쓰레기를 분리하는지 알고 싶어.
W: 왜냐면 각기 다른 재료에 맞춰 다른 재활용 공장이 있기 때문이지. 우리가 이렇게 분리를 하면 많은 사람들의 시간을 절약할 수 있어.

Word Review   p.66

1. digestion	2. rubbish
3. swallow	4. litter
5. mean	6. disturb
7. punish	8. socialize
9. at a time	10. switch off
11. in trouble	12. such as

Chapter 4
Technology
/ Content-Identifying Relationship

Overview   p.70

Sample Question: (D)

Basic Drills 1   p.72

1. (A)   2. (C)   3. (B)

1.
W: Look at what I got. It's a video camera.
M: Wow, it's so small! I thought it was a cell phone. Is that the smallest camera right now?
W: Yes, the man said that it is the smallest camera now.
M: I wish my video camera were small, too. Mine is like a schoolbag.

W: 내가 뭘 샀는지 봐. 비디오 카메라야.
M: 와, 정말 작다! 난 휴대폰인줄 알았어. 이게 요즘 제일 작은 카메라니?
W: 그래, 현재 가장 작은 카메라라고 그랬어.
M: 내 비디오 카메라도 작았으면 좋겠다. 내 카메라는 책가방만해.

2.   Typewriters can only type words on paper. It is noisy, and we cannot erase mistakes on typewriters. Computers are much more convenient. We can do a lot of things with a computer. It is much quieter than typewriters, and we can also correct mistakes easily.

타자기는 종이에만 글자를 칠 수 있다. 타자기는 소리가 나고 잘못된 부분을 지울 수도 없다. 컴퓨터는 훨씬 더 편리하다. 우리는 컴퓨터로 많은 일을 한다. 컴퓨터는 타자기보다 훨씬 조용하고 쉽게 수정할 수도 있다.

3. Airplanes are faster than helicopters. This is because the airplane has a jet engine, and a helicopter has a motor. The jet engine only needs to push the airplane quickly in one direction. The motor of the helicopter needs to turn a blade and make sure the helicopter does not fall from the sky.

비행기는 헬리콥터보다 빠르다. 비행기에는 제트 엔진이 있고 헬리콥터는 모터가 있기 때문이다. 제트 엔진은 비행기를 한 방향으로 빠르게 추진 시키기만 하면 된다. 헬리콥터의 모터는 헬리콥터의 날개를 돌려서 헬리콥터가 공중에서 떨어지지 않도록 하면 된다.

Basic Drills 2 p.73

| 1. (A)   2. (B)   3. (A) |

1. Car companies are always working hard to make our cars safer every day. Old cars were not very safe. Some old cars did not even have seatbelts. Cars today are designed and tested very hard to make sure that the people inside the car do not get hurt.

자동차 회사는 우리가 타는 자동차를 좀 더 안전하게 만들기 위해 항상 열심히 연구한다. 이전의 차들은 그리 안전하지 않았다. 어떤 구형 차들은 안전 벨트도 없었다. 오늘날의 차들은 차에 탄 사람이 다치지 않도록 하기 위해 열심히 테스트를 한다.

2. Motorboats and sailboats are very different. Motorboats have big engines to push them in the water. Sailboats have no engine and need wind to push them.

모터보트와 범선은 전혀 다르다. 모터보트는 물 속에서 큰 엔진이 보트를 밀어준다. 범선은 엔진이 없고 배를 밀어줄 바람만 필요하다.

3. Phones are getting smaller and lighter every day. Older cell phones were much bigger than modern ones. Old cell phones were as big as a book. People often joked about using cell phones as a weapon.

전화기는 날마다 작아지고 가벼워지고 있다. 오래된 휴대폰은 요즘의 것들보다 훨씬 더 크다. 옛날 휴대폰들은 책만큼 컸다. 사람들은 휴대폰을 무기로 사용한다는 농담을 종종 했었다.

Listening Practice ❶ p.74

| 1. (C)   2. (A) |

In 1966, Ralph Baer made the first video game called Pong. It was a very simple game. Modern games are very different from Pong because they are hard to play. Why are modern video games this way?

One reason is because people want better and real-looking games. Real-looking games mean that players need to think a lot and take longer to finish. Older video games got boring quickly because the games were very short and easy to finish.

Another reason is because game machines are getting more powerful. Game makers need powerful machines to make better games. This is why machines are very powerful.

1966년 랄프 베어는 Pong이라고 불리는 최초의 비디오 게임을 개발했다. 그것은 아주 단순한 게임이었다. 현대 게임은 Pong과는 전혀 달라서 게임을 하기가 어렵다. 현대의 비디오 게임은 왜 이런 것일까?

첫 번째 이유는 사람들이 더 좋고 진짜 같은 게임을 원하기 때문이다. 실감나는 게임은 사용자가 많은 생각을 해야 하고, 게임을 끝내는데 더 시간이 걸린다는 것을 의미한다. 이전 게임들은 게임이 아주 짧고 끝내기 쉽기 때문에 금방 지겨워졌다.

또 다른 이유는 게임기가 더 강력해졌기 때문이다. 게임 제작사는 더 나은 게임을 만들기 위해 더 강력한 게임기를 원했다. 그렇기 때문에 게임기계가 강력한 것이다.

Listening Practice ❷ p.75

| 1. (A)   2. (C) |

M: I need to buy a new computer.
W: Which computer are you going to buy?
M: I am still trying to decide between the Pentium

and AMD. I can't seem to make up my mind.
W: Yes, you are right. It is a hard choice to make. AMD seems to be quicker when it comes to games. Pentium is a little slower, but better for other programs.
M: Well, I do enjoy playing games, but the computer will be for homework and the internet. Maybe the Pentium is better for me, but it is more expensive. Oh, I don't know what I should do.

M: 컴퓨터를 새로 사야겠어.
W: 어떤 컴퓨터를 사려고 하는데?
M: 펜티엄과 AMD 둘 중에서 정하려고 하는 중이야. 결정을 못 내릴 것 같아.
W: 그래, 맞아. 선택하기 어렵겠구나. 게임을 할 때는 AMD가 더 빠르지. 펜티엄은 조금 느려. 하지만 다른 프로그램에서는 더 나아.
M: 글쎄, 난 게임을 정말 좋아하지만 컴퓨터는 숙제와 인터넷을 할 때 쓸 거거든. 어쩌면 나한텐 펜티엄이 더 낫겠다, 그렇지만 더 비싸. 아, 어떻게 해야 할 지 모르겠다.

Listening Practice ❸   p.76

1. (A)   2. (B)

Today, we watch television or use the internet for programs or news. But long ago, there was only radio.
Many people listened to the radio. The radio provided families with music and entertainment. Families would sit around and listen to the radio. Old radios only had one channel. Modern families can change channels on the TV very easily.
Radio stations also had drama and comedy shows. Radio stars read scripts with emotion as if the action was happening. There would be other people making background effects to make the show sound real. As a result, listeners used their imagination to "see" the drama in their heads.

오늘날 우리는 프로그램이나 뉴스를 접하기 위해 텔레비전을 보거나 인터넷을 이용한다. 하지만 오래 전에는 라디오뿐이었다.
많은 사람들은 라디오를 들었다. 라디오는 많은 가족들에게 음악과 오락거리를 제공했다. 가족들은 둘러앉아 라디오를 들었다. 옛날 라디오에는 채널이 하나 밖에 없었다. 현대의 가족들은 TV 채널을 아주 쉽게 바꿀 수 있다.
라디오 방송국에도 드라마나 코미디 프로그램이 있었다. 라디오 배우는 실제 그 일이 일어나고 있는 것처럼 감정을 실어 대본을 읽었다. 다른 사람들은 쇼가 실감나게 들리도록 배경 효과를 만들었다. 그 결과, 청취자들은 상상력을 발휘해 머릿속으로 드라마를 볼 수 있었다.

Listening Practice ❹   p.77

1. (B)   2. (B)

M: Do you remember the times when we didn't have cell phones?
W: Yeah. That was such a long time ago. It was so hard to meet someone outside. We couldn't call to say we were late, or if we wanted to change location.
M: Oh, it wasn't that bad. In fact, I miss those days. I get too many phone calls now.
W: Think about it. Cell phones are so important in emergencies. What would we do if we didn't have cell phones?
M: There were always emergencies even before cell phones. We had a lot more public phones.

M: 우리가 휴대폰이 없었던 시절이 기억나니?
W: 그럼. 진짜 오래 전 일이야. 밖에서 사람을 만나기가 참 어려웠어. 늦거나 장소를 바꾸겠다고 전화도 못하고.
M: 뭐, 그렇게 나쁘진 않았어. 사실 그 때가 그리워. 요즘은 전화가 너무 많이 와.
W: 생각해봐. 비상시에 휴대폰은 아주 중요해. 휴대폰이 없다면 어떻게 하겠니?
M: 휴대폰이 없던 때에도 비상상황은 항상 있었어. 공중 전화도 더 많았고.

iBT Practice ①   p.78

1. (B)   2. (C)   3. (A)   4. (A)
5. (C)   6. (D)

1-3.

Listen to the conversation between two friends.

W: It's amazing how everything is electronic.

M: Yes, because of the "microchip," things are much smaller now, and computers are quicker. Computers used to be slow and big.

W: What's a microchip?

M: It's a brain for machines. Nearly every electronic machine has a microchip. It's a small but very important part of machines.

W: Just how small is it? And when was it made?

M: Modern chips can be as small as a dot. They were first invented in 1959 by a company called "Texas Instruments." The inventor received a Nobel Prize.

W: I think he really deserved the prize. Without microchips, we would not have a lot of things we use every day.

W: 모든 것이 전자 관련 제품이라는 것이 놀라워.

M: 그래, 마이크로칩 덕분에 이제 제품들은 더 작아지고 컴퓨터는 더 빨라졌어. 예전 컴퓨터들은 느리고 컸었는데.

W: 마이크로칩이 뭐야?

M: 기계의 두뇌 같은 거지. 거의 모든 전자 제품은 마이크로칩을 갖고 있어. 그건 작지만 아주 중요한 기계 부품이야.

W: 정확히 얼마나 작은데? 그리고 언제 만들어진 건데?

M: 현대의 칩들은 점만큼 작아. 1959년 'Texas Instruments'라는 곳에서 처음 발명되었어. 발명자는 노벨상을 받았지.

W: 상을 받을 만 하네. 마이크로칩이 없으면 우리가 매일 사용하는 많은 것들을 못 가졌을 거야.

4-6.

Listen to the conversation between two students.

W: What are some uses of the internet?

M: I use it for email, playing games, and chatting with friends.

W: Do you know that the internet saves lives in hospitals too?

M: How is that possible? Do you mean that doctors share information online?

W: That is partly correct. Also, doctors in another country can operate on patients over the internet. A doctor on the other side of the world can control a robot using special sticks.

M: Are you serious? The robot actually does the surgery? That sounds dangerous. What if something goes wrong?

W: They have tested it for many years now and is proven safe. They only use it for emergencies if the patient needs the operation quickly. They say it is like any operation, but without the doctor.

W: 인터넷의 용도에는 어떤 것들이 있을까?

M: 난 이 메일을 보내거나 게임을 하거나 친구와 채팅을 할 때 사용해.

W: 병원에서는 인터넷이 생명을 구한다는 거 알고 있니?

M: 어떻게 그럴 수 있지? 의사들이 온라인으로 정보를 공유한다는 얘기니?

W: 부분적으로는 맞아. 또한 다른 나라의 의사들이 인터넷을 통해 환자를 수술 할 수도 있지. 지구 반대편에 있는 의사는 특수한 스틱을 이용해서 로봇을 조종할 수 있어.

M: 정말이야? 정말로 로봇이 수술을 한다고? 위험할 것 같은데. 뭐가 잘못되기라도 하면 어떡해?

W: 지금까지 몇 년 동안 시험을 거쳐왔고 안전하다고 입증됐어. 환자가 신속하게 수술을 받아야 하는 비상시에만 사용하는 거야. 의사만 없지 다른 수술과 마찬가지라고 해.

iBT Practice 2   p.80

1. (C)   2. (B)   3. (D)   4. (B)
5. (A)   6. (C)

1-3.

Listen to the student in a classroom.

The first photograph was taken in 1837. Digital cameras were invented in 1986 by Kodak. We can also find cameras in our cell phones. Cameras are now part of our lives.

Digital cameras can store many pictures in memory. Users can choose to take many pictures, and only keep the pictures that they need. Older cameras did not store pictures; they used film. The number of pictures depended on what kind of film the user had.

Digital cameras are cheap to maintain. They have no film to buy and develop like older cameras. Digital cameras only need a computer to download the pictures. This makes it cheap and easy for people to share their pictures and video on the internet.

최초의 사진은 1837년 촬영되었다. 디지털 카메라는 1986년 코닥에 의해 발명되었다. 핸드폰에서도 카메라를 볼 수 있다. 카메라는 이제 생활의 일부가 되었다.

디지털 카메라는 메모리에 많은 사진을 저장할 수 있다. 사용자는 많은 사진을 찍고 선택해서 필요한 사진만 간직하면 된다. 옛날 카메라는 사진을 저장하지 못하고 필름을 사용했다. 사진의 수는 사용하는 필름의 종류에 달려있었다.

디지털 카메라는 유지비가 저렴하다. 옛날 카메라처럼 현상해야 할 필름이 없다. 디지털 카메라는 사진을 다운로드하기 위한 컴퓨터만이 필요하다. 따라서 사람들은 사진과 동영상을 쉽고 저렴하게 인터넷에서 공유한다.

4-6.

Listen to the teacher in the classroom.

Some people like big cars. Others like good-looking cars. Many people love really fast sports cars. Do you know what is the fastest sports car in the world?

The McLaren F1 from England is the fastest sports car in the world. It was made in 1991. It can go nearly 400 kilometers per hour. Only 100 were made. It took more than a year to make one car. Even today, the F1 is the fastest car in the world.

Why is the car so fast? The engine is very powerful, and the car is very light. The shape of the car is also designed to go very quickly. This is why the car is so fast.

어떤 사람들은 큰 차를 좋아하고 어떤 사람들은 예쁜 차를 좋아한다. 많은 사람들은 정말 빠른 스포츠카를 좋아한다. 세상에서 가장 빠른 스포츠카가 무언지 알고 있는가?

영국의 McLaren F1이 세상에서 가장 빠른 스포츠카이다. 이 차는 1991년 만들어졌다. 거의 시속 400킬로까지 갈 수 있고 단지 100대만 만들었다. 차 한 대를 만드는데 일년이 넘게 걸린다. 오늘날 까지도 F1은 세상에서 가장 빠른 차이다.

왜 그 차는 그렇게 빠른 것 일까? 엔진이 아주 강력하고 차체가 가볍기 때문이다. 자동차 모양도 빨리 갈 수 있도록 디자인 되어있다. 그래서 그렇게 빠른 것이다.

Word Review p.86

1. maintain
2. imagination
3. erase
4. surgery
5. deserve
6. invent
7. emotion
8. weapon
9. provided ... with ...
10. depend on
11. between ... and ...
12. made up her mind

Chapter 5
History
/ Stance/Attitude

Overview   p.90

Sample Question: (C)

Basic Drills 1   p.92

1. (B)   2. (A)   3. (C)

1. W: Did you see the TV show about French history last night?
   M: Yes, I did, but it wasn't interesting to me. The story was so slow, and things didn't really happen until the end. I thought there would be more fighting and guns.
   W: Me, too. I thought it was boring too. We should have watched something else.

   W: 어제 밤에 프랑스 역사에 관한 TV 프로 봤니?
   M: 응, 봤어. 하지만 난 별로 재미 없던데. 이야기도 너무 느리고 끝까지 아무 일도 일어나지 않았잖아. 난 전투나 총기 장면이 더 나올 줄 알았는데.
   W: 나도 그랬어. 내 생각에도 지루했던 것 같아. 다른걸 볼 걸 그랬다.

2. W: Today is Korea's Independence Day. I'm so excited.
   M: Yes, it is. Can you imagine what the people felt at that time? There must have been big parties around the country.
   W: Yes, I'm sure the people would have celebrated.

   W: 오늘은 광복절이야. 너무 신나.
   M: 그래. 그 당시 사람들 기분이 어땠을까 상상이 가니? 전국에 큰 잔치가 열렸을 게 분명해.
   W: 그래, 분명 온 국민이 축하했을 거야.

3. W: Something looks funny about your pants. Did you do something?
   M: I didn't do anything. I only did some stretching exercises. I can't see anything wrong.
   W: Oh, now I know what's wrong. Your pants are torn! You must have stretched too hard. It looks so funny!
   M: Oh, no!

   W: 네 바지 어딘가 이상해 보여. 뭘 한 거야?
   M: 아무 것도 안 했어. 그냥 스트레칭을 좀 했을 뿐이야. 난 아무 이상이 없는 것 같은데.
   W: 아, 이제 뭐가 잘못됐는지 알겠다. 바지가 찢어졌잖아! 너무 열심히 스트레칭을 했나 보다. 너무 웃겨!
   M: 아! 이런.

Basic Drills 2   p.93

1. (B)   2. (B)   3. (A)

1. W: Have you heard of Bigfoot?
   M: No, what is it?
   W: It looks like a human, but is about 3 meters tall and very hairy. Some people say that they saw it in the woods. It lives in cold places.
   M: I do not believe in that kind of story.

   W: '빅풋'이라고 들어봤니?
   M: 아니, 그게 뭔데?
   W: 사람처럼 생겼는데, 키가 3미터 정도 되고 털이 아주 많대. 숲에서 봤다고 하는 사람들도 몇 명 있고. 추운 지방에서 살아.
   M: 난 그런 이야기는 믿지 않아.

2. The pyramids in Egypt are very large and have many drawings. These drawings are a picture language. Scientists and historians only understand a little bit of the language. This is because the picture language is very hard to understand and we know very little about the ancient Egyptians.

   이집트에 있는 피라미드는 아주 크고 많은 그림이 그려져 있다. 이 그림들은 그림문자이다. 과학자들과 역사학자들도 이 언어의 아주 일부만 이해할 수 있다. 왜냐하면 그림 문자는 이해하기 힘들고 우리가 고대 이집트인들에 대해 아는 것이 거의 없기 때문이다.

3. The Bermuda Triangle is near the east coast of America. Ships and airplanes disappeared in the triangle. The triangle is an area that can be drawn on a map. Scientists are not sure why ships and planes disappear, but they guess it is because compasses somehow point the wrong way in the triangle.

버뮤다 삼각지대는 미국 동부해안 부근에 있다. 선박과 비행기가 이 삼각지대에서 실종되었다. 이 지대는 지도 위에 그릴 수 있다. 과학자들은 왜 선박과 비행기가 사라졌는지 확실히 알 수는 없지만 어떤 알 수 없는 이유로 나침반이 삼각지대에서 잘못된 방향을 가리키기 때문이 아닐까 추측한다.

Listening Practice ❶ p.94

1. (C)   2. (B)

I'd like to talk about the tsunami in Southeast Asia. I was shocked to hear about the news, just like everyone else. Many countries were hit, but two countries had the most damage.

Indonesia was badly damaged by the tsunami. When the tsunami started there, at least 120,000 people died. Whole towns were washed away. The waves came into the towns and destroyed everything, including the trees and roads.

Sri Lanka also got hit by the tsunami. About 30,000 people died in the tsunami. Even the shape of the country changed. Nothing could survive the giant deadly waves.

동남아시아의 쓰나미에 관해 얘기해 보고자 한다. 그 소식을 듣고 나도 다른 사람들처럼 큰 충격을 받았다. 많은 나라를 강타했지만 두 나라가 가장 많은 피해를 입었다.

인도네시아 사람들은 쓰나미 때문에 큰 피해를 입었다. 쓰나미가 처음 그곳에서 발생했을 때 최소 12만 명의 사람이 사망했고, 마을 전체가 떠내려갔다. 파도가 마을을 침범해서 나무와 길을 포함한 모든 것을 파괴했다.

스리랑카 역시 쓰나미의 타격을 받았다. 약 3만 명의 사람들이 쓰나미에 의해 목숨을 잃었다. 나라의 모양까지도 변해버렸다. 그 거대하고 치명적인 파도 앞에서는 아무것도 살아남을 수 없었다.

Listening Practice ❷ p.95

1. (A)   2. (B)

W: What do you know about the Statue of Liberty?
M: I heard that the French gave it to America as a present.
W: 🎧 That's good. Did you also know that the statue is actually brown?
M: Excuse me? It looks green from all the pictures that I see.
W: The French used copper, which is light brown. Copper is a type of metal. Air and sea water changed the color.
M: So when did the statue turn green?
W: When the statue arrived in New York, it was very dark brown. About 20 years later, the statue turned into a light green color.

W: 넌 자유의 여신상에 대해 얼마나 알고 있니?
M: 프랑스가 미국에 선물로 준거라고 들었어.
W: 잘 아네. 그 여신상이 원래는 갈색이라는 것도 아니?
M: 뭐라고? 내가 보는 사진에서는 전부 초록색으로 보이던데.
W: 프랑스 사람들은 구리를 썼는데 그건 옅은 갈색이야. 구리는 금속의 일종이고, 공기와 바닷물 때문에 색이 변했지.
M: 그럼 언제 그 여신상이 초록색이 된 거야?
W: 여신상이 뉴욕에 도착했을 때는 아주 어두운 갈색이었어. 약 20년 후에 조각상은 옅은 초록색으로 변했어.

Listening Practice ❸ p.96

1. (C)   2. (B)

T: Has anyone heard of the space race?
M: I beg your pardon?
W: I know. It was a race between Russia and America to discover more about space.
T: That's correct. 🎧 The Russians won the first race, to send a man to space.
M: I can't believe that the Americans lost.

T: That's right. The Americans had plans to send a man to space too.
W: But I thought an American, Neil Armstrong, was the first man in space.
T: Some people think that he was the first man in space, but it is not true. He was the first man to walk on the moon. The Americans won that race.
M: And I think the Russians would have been upset with that news.

T: '우주 경쟁'이란 말 들어본 사람?
M: 뭐라고 말씀하셨어요?
W: 알아요. 러시아와 미국이 우주를 더 많이 탐험하기 위해 했던 경쟁이에요.
T: 맞았어. 러시아 사람들이 우주에 사람을 보내는 첫 번째 경쟁에서 이겼지.
M: 미국이 졌다는 게 안 믿어져.
T: 맞아. 미국인들도 우주에 인간을 보낼 계획을 갖고 있었어.
W: 하지만 미국인 닐 암스트롱이 우주에 간 첫 번째 사람인걸로 알았는데.
T: 몇몇 사람들이 그가 우주에 간 첫 번째 인간이라고 생각을 하지만 사실은 아니야. 그는 처음으로 달에 착륙해서 달 위를 걸은 사람이야. 미국인이 그 경쟁에서는 이긴 거야.
M: 그 소식을 듣고 러시아인들도 화가 났겠네요.

Listening Practice 4 p.97

1. (B)   2. (D)

Have you heard of the Panama Canal that changed the world? The canal cuts between North and South America. Why did people build the canal?

The canal saved time. Before the canal, ships had to sail around America to go from one end of America to the other. The canal saved many days and weeks of travel.

The canal also made traveling safer. Seas can be very dangerous, and ships cannot avoid storms. There was also less danger of pirates. Panama was well known for pirates at that time.

세상을 바꾼 파나마 운하에 대해 들어 본 적 있는가? 파나마 운하는 북미와 남미 사이를 관통한다. 왜 사람들은 운하를 만들었을까?

파나마 운하는 시간을 절약하게 했다. 운하를 만들기 전에는 선박이 미대륙 한쪽 끝에서 반대편 끝까지 가려면 돌아가야 했었다. 파나마 운하는 많은 항해 날짜를 절약할 수 있도록 했다.

또한 파나마 운하는 항해를 더 안전하게 했다. 바다는 아주 위험한 곳이고 배는 폭풍우를 피할 수 없다. 또 해적의 위험도 줄일 수 있었다. 그 당시 파나마는 해적들로 유명했었다.

iBT Practice 1 p.98

1. (C)   2. (C)   3. (B)   4. (A)
5. (A)   6. (D)

1-3.

Listen to the conversation between two students.

W: Do you know anything about the Berlin Wall?
M: Excuse me?
W: The Berlin Wall.
M: I only know it was in Berlin.
W: That wall used to divide East and West Germany. The Berlin Wall was destroyed in 1989.
M: Wow. Many people must have been interested in it.
W: Yes, it was very big news. East Germany was very poor. Their economy was very bad. They were not like West Germany.
M: What do you mean, not like West Germany?
W: West Germany's economy was one of the world's best. The whole world liked West German products.
M: So what happened when they joined?
W: A lot of people were afraid that Germany would face problems. West Germany had to use a lot of money to balance the two economies. But at the end, they were successful, and now there is only one Germany.

W: 베를린 장벽에 대해 알고 있니?
M: 뭐라고?
W: 베를린 장벽 말이야.
M: 그게 베를린에 있다는 것 밖에 몰라.
W: 그건 동독과 서독을 나누는 장벽이었어. 베를린 장벽은

1989년에 허물어졌지.
M: 와, 많은 사람들이 관심 있게 지켜봤겠다.
W: 그래, 아주 큰 뉴스였어. 동독은 아주 가난했었지. 경제 사정이 아주 좋지 않았어. 서독 같지가 않았지.
M: 서독 같지 않다니 무슨 말이야?
W: 서독의 경제력은 세계 최고 수준이었어. 전 세계가 서독의 상품을 좋아했었어.
M: 그럼 통일 이후에 무슨 일이 있었어?
W: 많은 사람들이 독일이 여러 문제에 직면할거라고 염려했었지. 서독은 두 나라의 경제 균형을 위해서 많은 돈을 써야만 했어. 결국엔 성공적이었고 지금은 하나의 독일만 존재하지.

4-6.

Listen to the teacher in the classroom.

The most famous and tallest pyramids are in Egypt. The pyramids were royal tombs of Pharaohs. 🎧 There are many things we do not understand about the pyramids, but we can find some answers by understanding the writings on the pyramids.

The pyramids are very hard to enter. They are like mazes. Some pyramids still have rooms that are unopened. The pyramids were designed this way because of grave robbers. Grave robbers stole the Pharaohs' gold and other things that were buried together.

The pyramids also have rooms for servants. The old Egyptians believed that the Pharaohs needed servants after they were dead, so they killed the Pharaohs' servants and buried them together in the pyramid.

가장 유명하고 높은 피라미드들은 이집트에 있다. 피라미드는 파라오의 왕릉이었다. 피라미드에 관해 알 수 없는 것들이 많이 있지만 피라미드에 쓰여진 글자들을 이해함으로써 몇 가지 해답을 알 수 있다.

피라미드를 들어가기는 매우 어렵다. 그것은 마치 미로 같다. 어떤 피라미드에는 아직까지도 열리지 않은 방들이 있다. 피라미드가 이런 식으로 디자인 된 것은 도굴범들 때문이었다. 도굴범들은 함께 묻혀있던 금과 다른 것들을 훔쳤다.

피라미드에는 하인을 위한 방도 있다. 고대 이집트인들은 파라오가 사후에도 하인이 필요할 것이라고 믿었기 때문에 파라오의 하인을 죽여서 피라미드 안에 함께 묻었다.

iBT Practice ② p.100

1. (B) 2. (B) 3. (A) 4. (B)
5. (A) 6. (D)

1-3.

Listen to the teacher in the classroom.

🎧 The Great Wall of China is so long that we can see it from space. It is the biggest thing that humans made. It is very long and tall. It is amazing to think that the wall was made over 2,000 years ago.

The walls were joined by the First Emperor of China to stop the Mongols. The original wall was about 5,000 kilometers.

More walls were built during the Han dynasty. This time, the walls had weapons and guard towers to fight with the enemies.

중국의 만리장성은 아주 길어서 우주에서도 볼 수 있다. 이것은 인간이 만든 가장 큰 것이다. 이 건물은 아주 길고 높다. 2천년 이전에 만들어진 장벽임을 생각해보면 놀라울 뿐이다.

이 장성은 진시황제에 의해서 몽골을 막기 위해 증축되었다. 원래 장벽의 길이는 5천 킬로미터 정도였다.

더 많은 장벽이 한나라 때에 건축되었다. 이때 그 벽들은 적들과 싸우기 위한 무기들과 감시탑들을 갖추었다.

4-6.

Listen to the conversation between two friends.

M: What have you heard about World War II?
W: I heard that Germany and Japan were part of the war.
M: Yes, but other countries were also part of the war. Germany and Japan were trying to have more power by controlling other countries.
W: Are you talking about Hitler?
M: Yes, he was a Nazi. The Nazis thought they were better than others, and killed a lot of people.
W: How about Japan? They fought with a lot of countries too.
M: Japan took over many countries, including Korea, China and other countries. They hurt people and forced them to learn about Japan. They also attacked the US.

W: So how did the war end?
M: 🎧 Germany finally lost the war, and Americans dropped two atom bombs in Japan. A total of 60 million people died in the war. Too many people died.

M: 2차 세계 대전에 대해 어떤 얘기를 들어봤니?
W: 독일과 일본이 가담했다는 건 들었어.
M: 그래, 하지만 다른 국가들도 전쟁에 가담했지. 독일과 일본은 다른 국가를 지배함으로써 더 많은 힘을 얻으려고 했어.
W: 히틀러 말하는 거니?
M: 그래, 그는 나치였어. 나치들은 그들이 다른 사람들 보다 우월하다고 믿고 많은 사람들을 학살했어.
W: 일본은? 그들도 많은 나라들과 싸웠잖아.
M: 일본은 한국, 중국을 포함한 다른 나라들을 빼앗았어. 그들은 사람들을 해치고 일본에 관해 배우도록 강요했어. 그들은 미국도 공격했지.
W: 그래서 전쟁은 어떻게 끝났니?
M: 독일이 결국 전쟁에서 졌고 미국이 일본에 두 개의 원자폭탄을 투하했어. 총 6천만 명의 사람들이 전쟁 중 사망했어. 너무 많은 사람들이 죽었지.

Word Review   p.106

1. divide	2. servant
3. royal	4. compass
5. maze	6. ancient
7. survive	8. pirate
9. is well known for	10. used to
11. washed away	12. is located in

Chapter 6
Biography
/ Function-Purpose

Overview   p.110

Sample Question: (B)

Basic Drills 1   p.112

1. (B)   2. (A)   3. (C)

1. M: I am going to the doctor tomorrow. I think I am going to need an operation.
   W: 🎧 What? What kind of operation?
   M: Just kidding. I'm only going in for a checkup.
   M: 나 내일 의사한테 갈 거야. 수술을 받아야 할 것 같아.
   W: 뭐? 무슨 수술인데?
   M: 농담이야. 그냥 건강진단만 받을 거야.

2. M: Could you tell me what time it is?
   W: I don't know. I'm busy. Go and ask someone else.
   M: 🎧 Well, excuse me for asking, then.
   M: 지금 몇 시인지 말해줄래?
   W: 몰라, 나 바빠. 다른 사람한테 가서 좀 물어봐.
   M: 음, 귀찮게 해서 미안.

3. W: How much did you study for the test?
   M: I have not even started studying yet. I have been sleeping the whole time.
   W: 🎧 Yeah, right. Your books and notes that you studied are everywhere.
   W: 시험 공부 얼마나 했니?
   M: 아직 공부 시작도 안 했어. 계속 잠만 잤어.
   W: 시치미 떼지마. 네가 공부한 책이랑 공책이 사방에 널려 있잖아.

Basic Drills 2 p.113

> 1. (A)   2. (B)   3. (A)

1. George Washington was the first President of the United States. He did many things to be fair to everyone. He even moved the capital from New York to Washington, D.C. What a leader he was!

   조지 워싱턴은 미합중국 최초의 대통령이었다. 그는 모든 사람에게 공평한 일들을 많이 했었다. 그는 수도를 뉴욕에서 워싱턴으로 옮기기까지 했다. 그는 정말 훌륭한 지도자였다!

2. Martin Luther King Jr. was a black leader that believed in peaceful protests. He was loved and respected by many people. There were other black leaders, but they did not believe in peace. Martin Luther King made sure his followers did not fight.

   마틴 루터 킹 2세는 평화적 저항을 믿는 흑인지도자였다. 많은 사람들은 그를 사랑하고 존경했다. 다른 흑인 지도자들도 많이 있었지만 그들은 평화를 믿지 않았다. 마틴 루터 킹은 그의 추종자들이 무력을 사용하지 않도록 했다.

3. Napoleon was a famous general of the French army. His army fought many battles with Spain and Austria. Napoleon won many wars. However, he made a mistake by fighting with Russia. He lost and his enemies sent him to a small island to live a quiet life after the war.

   나폴레옹은 프랑스 군대의 유명한 장군이었다. 그의 군대는 많은 전투에서 스페인과 오스트리아와 싸웠다. 나폴레옹은 많은 전쟁에서 승리하였다. 그러나 그가 러시아와 싸운 것은 실수였다. 전쟁에서 패한 후 적군은 그를 작은 섬으로 보내고 조용히 살게 했다.

Listening Practice 1 p.114

> 1. (A)   2. (D)

Abraham Lincoln is one of the most famous presidents of America. He did many things to make a difference in the United States. One of them was to free the slaves.

When Lincoln was president, there were many people using slaves. Lincoln stopped people from using slaves. The South was unhappy and started a fight. The North and South had a big war. Lincoln won the war in the end.

Lincoln was killed while watching a play. A man shot Lincoln in the head. Many people were sad by Lincoln's death. Even today, people still remember Abraham Lincoln as a great man.

아브라함 링컨은 미국의 유명한 대통령들 중 하나이다. 그는 미국을 바꾸기 위해 많은 일들을 했다. 그 중 하나가 노예를 해방한 것이다.

링컨이 대통령이었을 때 많은 사람들이 노예를 부렸다. 링컨은 사람들의 노예 이용을 중지 시켰다. 남부사람들은 불만을 갖고 전쟁을 시작했다. 북부와 남부는 큰 전쟁을 했다. 결국에는 링컨이 승리했다.

링컨은 연극을 보던 중 사망했다. 한 남자가 링컨의 머리를 총으로 쏘았다. 많은 사람들은 링컨의 죽음에 슬퍼했다. 아직까지도 사람들은 아브라함 링컨을 위대한 인물로 기억한다.

Listening Practice 2 p.115

> 1. (C)   2. (B)

W: I just came back from Paris.
M: Really? How was your trip?
W: It was great. I got to see the Eiffel Tower.
M: That's wonderful! Was it beautiful?
W: Oh yes, it was very beautiful. Did you know that the French did not want the tower? People thought that the tower made up of metal would look ugly.
M: Yes, but after it was built, people thought it was beautiful.
W: Yes. Oh, did you know that the builder, Gustave Eiffel, also helped build the Statue of Liberty? Wasn't he a great man to do such things?
M: Wow, I didn't know that. I guess you learned a lot of things in Paris.

W: 나 방금 파리에서 돌아왔어.
M: 정말? 여행은 재미있었어?

W: 굉장했어! 에펠탑도 봤어.
M: 대단하다! 멋있었니?
W: 그럼, 너무 아름다웠어. 너 프랑스 사람들이 에펠탑을 원하지 않았다는 거 알았니? 사람들은 금속으로 된 탑이 추할 거라고 생각했대.
M: 하지만 다 만들고 나서는 사람들이 아름답다고 생각했지.
W: 맞아. 아, 그 건축가 구스타프 에펠이 자유의 여신상을 만드는데 참여했다는 거 알아? 그런 일들을 하다니 정말 대단하지 않니?
M: 와, 그건 몰랐다. 파리에서 많이 배워온 것 같구나.

Listening Practice ❸ p.116

1. (B)   2. (A)

Let's talk about a very famous artist today. There are many artists in this world, but Pablo Picasso is the most famous. No other artist has been so famous while he was alive. Even Leonardo da Vinci was not as famous when he was alive. 🎧 Picasso drew art that did not look normal, but many people liked Picasso's work. He made a new type of art called "cubism." Many people wanted to buy his paintings. Does everyone follow?
Picasso's art pieces were expensive. His art got even more expensive when he died. There might never be another great artist like Picasso.

오늘은 아주 유명한 예술가 얘기를 해보자. 세계에 많은 예술가들이 있지만 파블로 피카소가 가장 유명하다. 다른 어떤 예술가들도 생전에 이렇게 유명한 적은 없었다. 레오나르도 다 빈치 조차도 살아 있을 때는 그만큼 유명하지 않았었다.
피카소는 다른 그림과는 다른 평범하지 않은 작품을 그렸지만 많은 사람들이 피카소의 작품을 좋아했다. 그는 '입체파'라고 불리는 새로운 형식을 만들었다. 많은 사람들이 그의 그림을 사고 싶어했다. 잘 알겠니?
피카소의 예술 작품은 비쌌다. 그의 예술작품은 사후에 훨씬 더 비싸졌다. 피카소 같이 위대한 예술가는 결코 없을 것이다.

Listening Practice ❹ p.117

1. (C)   2. (B)

W: Do you remember Mother Theresa?
M: Of course I do. 🎧 Don't you think she was great?
W: Yes, I think so. The things she did were great.
M: I was surprised to hear that she came from a wealthy family. She had the chance to live a comfortable life. Instead, she chose to use all her money to help the poor.
W: Yes, she had so much love that she gave up everything to help the poor. She helped those that even hospitals did not want.
M: Thanks to her, there are many countries that follow her example and help the poor in their own land.

W: 테레사 수녀 기억나니?
M: 당연히 기억나지. 대단하지 않니?
W: 그래, 그런 것 같아. 그녀가 한 일들은 대단했어.
M: 그녀가 부유한 집안에서 태어났다는 소리를 듣고 깜짝 놀랐어. 편안한 삶을 살 수도 있었는데. 그대신 자기 생을 모두 가난한 사람들을 돕고 함께 살기 위한 길을 선택한 거잖아.
W: 그래, 넘치는 사랑으로 모든 것을 포기하고 가난한 사람들을 도왔지. 병원에서도 받아주지 않는 사람들을 도와 주었어.
M: 덕분에 그녀의 모범을 본받아서 가난한 사람들을 돕는 나라가 많이 있어.

iBT Practice 1 p.118

1. Yes: (A), (B) / No: (C), (D)   2. (A)
3. (C)   4. (C)
5. Yes: (A), (B) / No: (C), (D)   6. (D)

1-3.
Listen to the teacher in the classroom.

The world's most important bicycle race is in France. The best bicycle riders from all over the world come to the race. Q2 🎧 The best well-known champion is Lance Armstrong. He won the race many times. But Lance Armstrong is also known for something else.

Lance Armstrong had cancer. Many doctors said that Lance could die. Lance did not give up and chose to fight the cancer. He went through a lot of hard treatment in hospital. It was very hard for Lance to fight, but he won. After that, he went to race. Since then, he has won six races.

Q3 🎧 Lance also started an organization called the Armstrong Foundation. The group helps other patients have a normal life. He is truly everyone's hero.

세계에서 가장 영향력 있는 자전거 경기는 프랑스에서 열린다. 최고의 자전거 선수들이 전 세계에서 경기를 하러 온다. 가장 유명한 챔피언은 랜스 암스트롱이다. 그는 여러 번 우승을 했다. 하지만 랜스 암스트롱은 다른 일로도 유명하다.

랜스 암스트롱은 암에 걸렸었다. 많은 의사들은 랜스가 죽을 수도 있다고 했다. 랜스는 포기하지 않고 암과 싸우기로 했다. 그는 병원에서 많은 힘든 치료를 견뎠다. 랜스가 견디기는 쉽지 않았지만 결국 그는 이겨냈다. 그 후 그는 경기에 나갔다. 그 이후로 여섯 번이나 우승을 했다.

랜스는 '암스트롱 재단'이라는 단체를 만들었다. 그 재단은 다른 환자들을 도와 정상적인 삶을 살도록 한다. 그는 모든 이들의 진정한 영웅이다.

4-6.

Listen to the conversation between two students.

M: Thomas Edison was an intelligent man. He invented so many things.

W: Isn't he the famous genius? How many things did he invent?

M: I heard that Edison and his electric company invented more than 1,000 inventions when Edison was alive.

W: Wow. That is a lot. What do you think is his most important invention?

M: It has to be the light bulb. Light bulbs are very important to us. We use them everywhere.

W: That is true. 🎧 I wonder what else he invented that we use every day.

M: Let's see. There are just so many.

W: I remember one. He invented the video camera. Without it, we would not have anything to watch on TV.

M: Yes, you're right. That was a very important invention too.

M: 토마스 에디슨은 똑똑한 사람이었어. 그는 많은 것들을 발명했지.

W: 그 사람 유명한 천재 아니야? 얼마나 많은 것을 발명했는데?

M: 에디슨과 그의 전기 회사가 에디슨이 살아있을 때만 천건 이상의 발명을 했다고 들었어.

W: 와, 많이 발명했다. 그 중에 제일 중요한 발명품이 뭐라고 생각해?

M: 전구겠지. 전구는 아주 중요하잖아. 어디서든 사용하고.

W: 맞아. 그가 발명한 것 중에 우리가 매일 사용하는 게 뭐가 또 있을까 궁금해.

M: 글쎄. 너무 많아.

W: 하나 기억났다. 비디오 카메라도 발명했어. 그게 없으면 TV에서 아무것도 볼 수 없을걸.

M: 그래, 맞아. 그것도 중요한 발명품이구나.

iBT Practice ② p.120

1. (C) 2. (D) 3. (A) 4. (A)
5. (B) 6. (D)

1-3.

Listen to the conversation between two friends.

W: Q2 🎧 Who is Nobel? I saw something on TV last night.

M: Don't you know about Alfred Nobel?

W: No, I don't. Who was he?

M: He was a Swedish inventor that made dynamite. Many companies needed dynamite, and so he was very successful.

W: His family must have been very happy about it.

M: He did not marry, so he didn't have a wife or kids. Q3 🎧 He decided to use all the money to set up the Nobel Prize.

W: Yeah, right.

M: It's true. He was sad to find out that dynamite was also used to kill people. He wanted to reward people who did great things for others.

W: 노벨이 누구니? 어젯밤 TV에서 뭘 봤는데.

M: 너 알프레드 노벨 모르니?

W: 아니 몰라. 그게 누군데?

M: 그 사람은 다이너마이트를 발명한 스웨덴 발명가였어. 많은 회사들이 다이너마이트가 필요했어. 그래서 그는 크게 성공

했지.
W: 그의 가족들도 많이 기뻤겠다.
M: 그 사람은 결혼하지 않았어. 그래서 부인도 자식도 없었지. 그는 그의 모든 돈을 노벨상을 만드는데 썼어.
W: 설마 그랬겠어.
M: 사실이야. 그는 다이너마이트가 사람을 죽이는데도 사용됐다는 것을 알고 슬펐어. 그는 다른 사람들을 위해 위대한 일을 한 사람들에게 상을 주고 싶어했지.

4-6.

Listen to the conversation between two friends.

W: How much do you know about General Lee? They say he did many great things.
M: Oh yes, everyone knows General Lee.
W: Really? Tell me more about him.
M: Q2 🎧 Well, he was a general of the Korean army a long time ago. He designed a ship.
W: Is that all? Anyone can draw a ship.
M: Q3 🎧 Not just any ship. General Lee made a special ship called the turtle ship. The outside was very strong, so the soldiers inside were safe. It was not like normal ships.
W: Now that you mention it, I do remember seeing a picture of the turtle ship. Does it have an angry turtle head on top of the ship?
M: Yes, those are the turtle ships. General Lee used the turtle ships to fight off the Japanese. That is why he is so famous.

W: 이순신 장군에 대해 얼마나 알고 있니? 많은 위대한 일을 했다고 하던데.
M: 그래, 맞아. 모든 사람이 이순신 장군을 알지.
W: 정말? 그 얘기 좀 더 해줘.
M: 글쎄, 그는 오래 전 한국 군대의 장군이었어. 그는 배를 하나 디자인했어.
W: 그게 다야? 누구나 배는 그릴 수 있잖아.
M: 그냥 배가 아니야. 이순신은 거북선이라고 하는 특별한 배를 만들었어. 겉은 아주 튼튼해서 그 안의 병사들은 안전했어. 보통 배랑은 달랐어.
W: 네가 그 얘기를 하니까 거북선 그림을 본 게 생각난다. 배 꼭대기에 험악한 거북이 머리가 있지 않니?
M: 그래, 그게 거북선이야. 이순신 장군은 거북선을 이용해서 일본군을 격퇴했어. 그래서 그렇게 유명한 거야.

Word Review   p.126

1. reward
2. protest
3. slave
4. general
5. normal
6. respect
7. follower
8. enemy
9. grew up
10. set up
11. give up
12. in the end

Mini Test 1

p.130

1. (C) 2. (A) 3. (B) 4. (D)
5. (D) 6. Yes: (B), (D) / No: (A), (C)
7. (C) 8. (D) 9. (B) 10. (A)
11. Yes: (A), (D) / No: (B), (C) 12. (D)

1-4.

Listen to the conversation between two students.

M: You look so tired today. What happened to you?

W: Oh, I went to bed late. I was playing a new computer game. It was fun when I was playing, but I'm so tired now. All I can think of is the game.

M: Didn't you know that we have a history test today? You should have studied, not played computer games. I studied a lot last night. This test is going to be very hard. It is going to be about Korean history.

W: Q3 🎧 Oh, no, I forgot about the test! I really wish I could go back in time to study. Quick, give me your notes.

M: It's too late now. Q4 🎧 The test starts in 10 minutes. Just pray that the test will be about the game.

M: 오늘 너 참 피곤해 보인다. 무슨 일 있었어?

W: 아, 늦게 잠들었어. 새로운 컴퓨터 게임을 했었거든. 게임할 때는 재미있었는데, 지금은 너무 피곤하다. 게임밖에 생각이 안나.

M: 오늘 역사 시험 보는 거 몰랐어? 너는 컴퓨터 게임이 아니라 공부를 해야 했어. 난 어젯밤에 공부 많이 했는데. 이번 시험은 아주 어려울 거야. 한국 역사에 관해 시험을 볼 거거든.

W: 오, 안돼. 시험에 대해 잊고 있었네! 과거로 시간을 되돌려서 공부할 수 있다면 좋겠다. 어서 네 노트 좀 줘봐.

M: 이제 너무 늦었어. 10분 후에 시험 시작이야. 그냥 게임에 관한 시험이 나오길 기도해라.

5-8.

Listen to the student in a classroom.

Fishing can be a fun hobby. But long-line fishing can be hard and dangerous work.

In long-line fishing, a boat travels in the ocean for a long time. Storms are always dangerous to the fishermen. When a storm comes, there is no safe place to go. The long-line fishermen must sail through the storm and hope for the best.

The fish that they catch are also very dangerous. They catch swordfish. Swordfish are very big and strong. They have a long sharp nose. If a swordfish cuts a fisherman, it can seriously hurt or even kill him. There is no hospital or doctor to help the long-line fishermen in the ocean. Long-line fishermen must always remember to be safe.

낚시는 즐거운 취미가 될 수 있다. 하지만 연승 낚시는 어렵고 위험할 수 있다.

연승 낚시를 하려면 보트가 오랫동안 바다에 있어야 한다. 낚시꾼들에게 폭풍은 언제나 위험하다. 바다에서 폭풍이 닥치면 안전하게 피할 곳이 없다. 연승 낚시꾼들은 폭풍을 헤치고 항해를 해야 하고 상황이 좋아지기를 바라는 수 밖에 없다.

그들이 잡는 고기들도 위험하다. 그들은 황새치를 잡는다. 황새치는 아주 크고 힘이 세다. 그들은 길고 날카로운 코를 가졌다. 황새치에게 베이면 심각하게 다치거나 심지어 죽을 수도 있다. 바다 한가운데는 그 낚시꾼을 도울만한 병원도 의사도 없다. 연승 낚시꾼들은 항상 안전에 유의해야 한다.

9-12.

Listen to the speaker.

Chocolate cakes look great and taste lovely. So how do people make chocolate cakes? It's easier than you might think.

We mix flour, eggs, milk and sugar together. We keep mixing these things together until it becomes what we call dough. We mix chocolate syrup or melted chocolate together with the dough.

Next, we put the dough into a pan. We put it into a hot oven and bake the dough for about 30 minutes. Remember to put it into a pretty pan, because the shape of the cake will be the shape of the pan.

🎧 After it is baked, we take out the cake, and

we decorate the cake by covering it with whipping cream and sprinkle some chocolate flakes on it. All that's left is to eat it!

초콜릿 케이크는 보기에도 좋고 맛도 아주 좋다. 그렇다면 사람들은 어떻게 초콜릿 케이크를 만드는 것일까? 그것은 우리가 생각하는 것보다 더 쉽다.

밀가루, 달걀, 우유와 설탕을 섞는다. 소위 반죽이 될 때까지 재료를 계속 섞는다. 초콜릿 시럽이나 녹인 초콜릿을 반죽과 함께 섞는다.

그 다음 반죽을 팬에 담는다. 예열된 오븐에 넣고 약 30분 동안 반죽을 굽는다. 케이크의 모양은 팬의 모양과 같아질 테니 예쁜 팬에 담는걸 잊지 말자.

다 구워지고 나면 케이크를 꺼내서 생크림이나 초콜릿 가루를 뿌려 장식을 한다. 이제 먹기만 하면 된다.

Mini Test 2

p.136

1. (D)	2. (C)	3. (B)	4. (A)
5. (A)	6. (B)	7. (C)	8. (A)
9. (D)	10. (A)	11. (B)	12. (C)

1-4.

Listen to the conversation between two friends.

W: Have you seen some of the funny fashions of the 60s?

M: I can only remember one from the movies that I saw. Everyone had really long hair. Some wore headbands. They looked awful.

W: Yup, that's one of them. I saw pictures of my mom and dad when they were young. They had that hairstyle, too.

M: I guess it was very fashionable back then. Not many people seemed to have short hair.

W: 🎧 Another one is pants with wide ends. You know those pants that look like bells at the ends.

M: Oh, not those! They say the wider the ends, the better it was. It is the funniest-looking fashion I have seen.

W: 60년대 우스꽝스러운 패션을 본 적이 있니?

M: 영화에서 봤던 게 하나 기억나는데. 모두들 머리가 정말 길었어. 어떤 사람들은 머리띠도 했고. 좀 그렇더라.

W: 그래, 그것도 60년대 패션 중 하나야. 우리 엄마랑 아빠 젊으셨을 때 사진을 봤는데 그 분들도 헤어스타일이 그랬어.

M: 그 당시에 아주 유행했었나 봐. 짧은 머리를 한 사람들은 별로 많은 것 같지 않더라.

W: 또 다른 패션 중에 끝부분이 넓은 바지가 있는데. 그 바지가 종모양으로 퍼지는 거 너도 알고 있지.

M: 아, 그건 정말 별로야. 끝부분이 넓을수록 좋은 거였다고 그러더라. 내가 본 것 중에 제일 웃기는 패션이야.

5-8.

Listen to the teacher in the classroom.

Computer games nowadays are very

advanced. Most teenagers like to play computer games. But computer games can be a very bad and big problem in society.

🎧 Computer games can take a lot of time to finish. Some computer games do not even have endings. The games try to copy real life. However, this takes away time from our real lives. We should control the amount of time we play games.

Computer games can also make younger children think that real life and games are the same. Some younger children copy the bad things in the computer games. Younger children try to understand what they see in games by doing it themselves. We should never follow what we see in games.

요즘 컴퓨터 게임은 많은 발전을 했다. 많은 십대들이 컴퓨터 게임 하기를 좋아한다. 하지만 컴퓨터 게임은 아주 크고 심각한 사회 문제가 될 수도 있다.

컴퓨터 게임을 끝내려면 많은 시간이 걸린다. 끝이 없는 컴퓨터 게임도 있다. 게임은 실제 삶을 모방하려고 한다. 그러나 이것은 우리의 실제 생활에서 시간을 빼앗아간다. 우리는 컴퓨터 게임을 하는 시간을 조절해야 한다.

컴퓨터 게임은 어린 아이들이 실제 생활과 게임이 같다고 생각하도록 할 수도 있다. 어떤 어린이들은 컴퓨터 게임에서 본 나쁜 짓들을 따라 한다. 어린 아이들은 게임 속에서 일어난 일들을 직접 행동해 봄으로써 게임을 이해하려고 한다. 절대로 게임에서 보는 것을 따라 해서는 안 된다.

9-12.

Listen to the teacher in the classroom.

In many countries, each family has at least one car. Cars use a lot of tires. What should we do with used tires? A long time ago, they burned the tires outside or stored them. There was no use for old tires. Thanks to technology, we can solve the problem in two ways.

We can burn the tires in special factories. In a special factory, machines catch the dangerous smoke from the tires. The heat from the burning tires makes electricity. This can help the environment.

We can also recycle tires in many ways by making something different. For example, we can cut up the recycled tires into small pieces and put them into new roads to make better roads.

많은 나라에서 각 가정에 적어도 한대의 차를 갖고 있다. 자동차는 많은 양의 타이어를 사용한다. 사용한 타이어로는 무엇을 해야 할까? 오래 전에는 밖에서 타이어를 태우거나 모아두었다. 오래된 타이어는 쓸모가 없었다. 기술의 발전덕분에 우리는 두 가지 방법으로 문제를 해결할 수 있다.

특수 공장에서 타이어를 태워버릴 수 있게 되었다. 이러한 공장에서는 기계가 타이어에서 나오는 유해한 연기를 모아 처리한다. 타이어를 태우면서 나는 열로 전기를 만든다. 이렇게 하면 환경에 도움을 줄 수 있다.

또 사용된 타이어로 다른 것을 만듦으로써 여러 가지로 재활용할 수 있다. 예를 들어 재활용 타이어를 작은 조각으로 잘라서 새 도로를 만드는데 넣어서 더 좋은 도로가 되도록 한다.

Mini Test 3

p.142

1. (C)	2. (A)	3. (C)	4. (D)
5. (C)	6. (A)	7. (D)	8. (B)
9. (D)	10. (B), (D) / No: (A), (C)		
11. (B)	12. (A)		

1-4.

Listen to the conversation between two friends.

M: How old do you think music videos are?

W: I think they are very old. We see them all the time on TV.

M: That's what people think. Music videos, however, are not really old.

W: What do you mean?

M: The Beatles made a movie to go with their song, but that was a full movie. The first true music video was by a singer called Mike Nesmith in 1981. The videos were short films for just one song.

W: That was when MTV was born. They must have been a very good match.

M: Yes. Music videos quickly became an important part of the music business. Singers still spend a lot of time and money making music videos. Many big stars can thank the music video for their success.

M: 뮤직비디오의 역사가 얼마나 될 것 같니?

W: 아주 오래 된 것 같은데. TV로 항상 보잖아.

M: 보통 그렇게 생각하지. 하지만 뮤직비디오는 그렇게 많이 오래 되지 않았어.

W: 무슨 소리야?

M: 비틀즈가 노래에 어울릴만한 영화를 만들었지만 그건 한편의 영화였어. 최초의 정식 뮤직비디오는 마이크 네스미스가 1981년에 만든 거야. 그 비디오는 한 곡의 음악만을 위한 짧은 영화였어.

W: 그때 MTV가 탄생했지. 그 둘이 (시기적으로) 아주 잘 맞아 떨어졌었겠다.

M: 맞아. 뮤직비디오는 급속하게 음악 산업에서 중요한 요소가 되었어. 가수들은 여전히 뮤직비디오를 만드는데 많은 시간과 돈을 투자해. 많은 대형 스타들은 그들의 성공이 뮤직비디오 덕이라고도 할 수 있어.

5-8.

Listen to the teacher in the classroom.

The original people of the United States are Indians, or Native Americans. When the Pilgrims reached America, the Indians were friendly and helped them.

The Pilgrims did not know anything about America when they first arrived. The natives showed them how to be warm in winter and grow food. The Pilgrims were friends with the Indians.

As time went by, a lot of the Native Americans' land was taken away by the white Americans. This made the Indians very angry, and they fought with the white Americans. There was a lot of fighting between the white and Native Americans.

The Indians were very brave, but they lost the war. They were forced to live in camps and not allowed to leave. Today, the Native Americans are free, and we can learn a lot about them.

미국의 원래 거주자들은 인디언, 혹은 아메리칸 원주민들이었다. 순례자들이 처음 미국에 도착했을 때, 인디언들은 호의적이었고 그들을 도왔다.

순례자들은 처음 도착했을 때 미대륙에 대해 전혀 알지 못했다. 원주민들이 겨울에 따뜻하게 지내는 법이나 농사 짓는 법들을 알려주었다. 순례자들은 인디언들의 친구였다.

시간이 지나면서 많은 아메리칸 원주민의 땅이 백인들에게 빼앗기게 된다. 이 때문에 인디언들은 아주 분개해서 백인들과 싸우게 된다. 백인과 아메리칸 원주민들 사이에 많은 전투가 있었다.

인디언들은 아주 용감했지만 전쟁에서 졌다. 그들은 강제로 캠프 안에서 생활해야만 했고 밖으로 나오지 못했다. 오늘날 아메리칸 원주민들은 해방되었고 우리는 그들에 대한 많은 것들을 알 수 있다.

9-12.

Listen to the speaker.

Genghis Khan was a great ruler of Mongolia long ago. Genghis Khan means Universal Ruler. He joined the separate groups in the country to form Mongolia.

Genghis Khan was a great fighter. His army

was very good with many weapons and riding horses. Most countries that went to war with the Mongols lost. This was why many countries were under Genghis Khan, from East Asia to parts of Europe. But were they bad people? Or were they good?

No, Genghis Khan was also a fair person. If his enemies gave up and served him, he treated them as his friends. He did not force them to change the way they lived to a Mongolian lifestyle.

칭기스칸은 오래 전 위대한 몽골의 통치자였다. 칭기스칸은 세계의 통치자라는 뜻이다. 그는 흩어진 부족들을 합쳐서 몽골을 만들었다.

칭기스칸은 위대한 전사였다. 그의 군은 많은 무기와 말을 타는데 익숙했다. 몽골과 싸운 대부분의 국가는 졌다. 그래서 동아시아에서 유럽에 이르는 많은 국가들이 칭기스칸 통치 아래 있었다. 하지만 그들은 나쁜 민족이었을까? 아니면 좋은 사람들인가?

칭기스칸은 공정한 사람이었다. 그의 적이 항복을 하고 그를 따르면 그는 그들을 친구로 대했다. 그는 그들이 살던 방식을 몽골 식으로 바꾸도록 강요하지 않았다.

LinguaForum TOEFL® iBT Series eBasic - e - b - b+ - m - i - Hooked On

Junior Series
- **iBT eBasic TOEFL®** Reading / Listening
- **iBT e TOEFL®** Reading / Listening / Grammar
- **iBT b TOEFL®** Reading / Listening / Writing / Grammar
- **iBT b+ TOEFL®** Reading / Listening

Test Prep.

Intermediate Level
- **TOEFL® iBT** m-Reading / m-Listening / m-Writing / m-Speaking
- **New Edition TOEFL® iBT** i-Reading / i-Listening / i-Writing / i-Speaking
- **TOEFL® iBT Core Topic Guide** Series / **Intro** Vocabulary

Advanced Level
- **New Edition Hooked On TOEFL®** Reading / Listening / Writing / Speaking
- **Frequency#1 TOEFL® Vocabulary**
- **TOEFL® iBT INSIDER** - The Super Guide / **TOEFL® iBT Test Book I**

LinguaForum™

🔍 시험 상세 : 시험 화면은 다음과 같이 구성되었습니다.

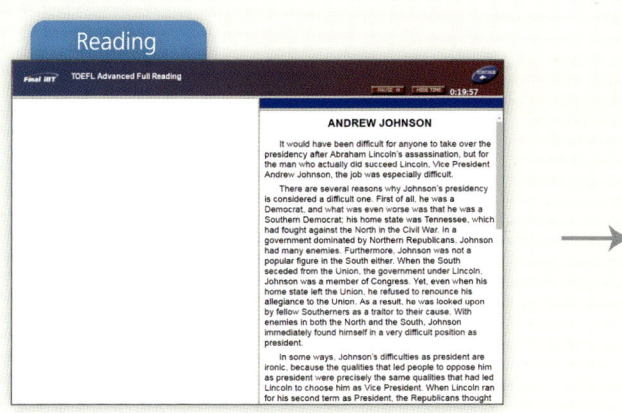

학술적인 내용의 지문을 이해하는 능력을 평가합니다.

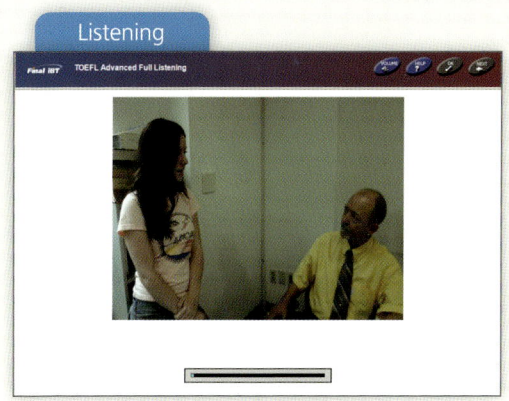

강의, 교실 토론 및 대화를 듣고 이해하는 능력을 평가합니다.

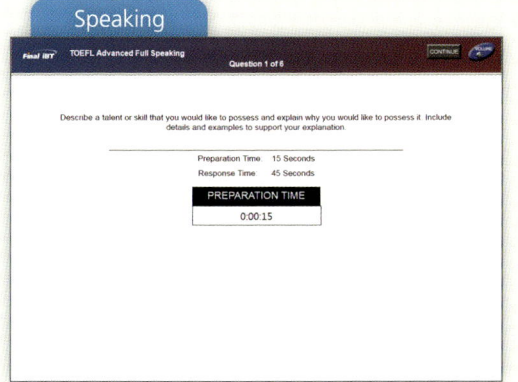

다양한 주제에 대해 말할 수 있는 능력을 평가합니다.

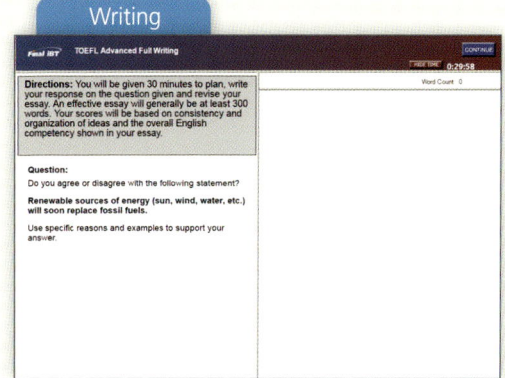

강의내용을 요약하고 자신의 의견을 정리하는 작문능력을 평가합니다.

각각의 모의 테스트를 마친 후 **예상점수를 확인**할 수 있습니다. SPEAKING과 WRITING 점수는 **채점 전문 인력**에 의해 매겨집니다.

시험 준비 세팅

먼저, 마이크가 있는 헤드셋을 준비해주세요.
그리고 인터넷이 연결된 상태에서 크롬브라우저로 접속하여 시험에 응시하시면 됩니다.

시험 응시 및 문의 사항 Tel : 02-3483-2786

초급부터 실전까지 토플교재의 바이블

링구아포럼 TOEFL Series

- 아시아 최초로 2003년부터 미국은 물론 전 세계로 영어 교재와 판권 수출
- 온라인 서점 아마존닷컴 토플 판매 1위 (2003년, 2004년)
- 주니어 토플 개념 정의
- 최초 6단계별 토플 시리즈 개발

링구아포럼의 6단계별 토플 교재 eBASIC / e / b / m / i / Hooked on / Insider / Test Book
- eBasic 시리즈를 시작으로 e, b, m, i, Hooked On 순으로 단계가 올라갑니다. 영문 종합서 Insider 와 모의고사집 Test Book이 있습니다.

1 단계 — New Edition eBasic Series
중학교 1~2학년 수준으로 토플을 처음 접하는 학습자를 위한 입문 단계로, iBT의 주제와 형식, 문제유형에 입문 수준의 어휘와 문법으로 구성되었습니다.

〈개정판〉

2 단계 — New Edition e Series
중학교 2~3학년 수준의 토플 학습자를 위해 개발된 두번째 초급 단계이며, iBT의 주제와 형식, 문제유형에 입문 수준의 어휘와 문법으로 구성되었습니다.

〈개정판〉

  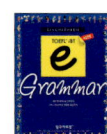 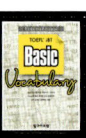

3 단계 — b Series
중학교 3학년 이상의 영어능력을 가진 학습자를 대상으로 개발. 링구아포럼 eBasic, e 시리즈를 학습한 학습자에서부터, 토플을 처음 접하는 대학생/성인들 모두 토플에 적응하고 중급~고급 단계로 진입할 수 있도록 구성 되었습니다.

4 단계 — m Series
중급 수준(성인 입문)의 토플 학습자를 대상으로 개발. iBT에 등장하는 모든 주제와 문제유형 등을 모두 다루었으며, 실전보다 조금 쉬운 수준으로 연습할 수 있습니다.

〈개정판〉

   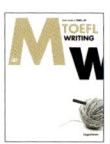 

5 단계 — New Edition i Series
실제 토플 시험을 준비하는 학습자를 대상으로 개발. 링구아포럼 토플 시리즈의 중/고급단계로, iBT에 등장하는 모든 주제와 문제유형 등을 모두 다루었으며, 실전과 거의 유사한 수준으로 연습할 수 있습니다.

6 단계 — New Edition Hooked On Series
실제 토플 시험을 준비하는 학습자를 대상으로 한 고급단계로, iBT에 등장하는 모든 주제와 문제유형등을 모두 다루어,실전과 동일한 수준으로 연습할 수 있습니다.

 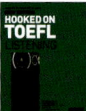